Español Con Amigos Dos

A Partner Approach to Learning
Intermediate Conversational Spanish

Author: Melissa J. O'Gara
Illustrator: Steve Hickner

ACKNOWLEDGMENTS

This book would not be possible without the love, support, and encouragement of my entire family. First and foremost I'd like to thank my parents, Sheldon and Marilyn Baker, for instilling in me the desire to learn about and understand different cultures of the world. I can not possibly express to both of them my gratitude for all they have done for me, but I can acknowledge that without their example and guidance, I would not have been able to travel and experience for myself the many beautiful cultures and people of the world. My entire education, including my ability to speak and write in Spanish, is because of their neverending support and love.

I also want to thank my husband, Michael, for his continual encouragement. Without his patience and willingness to hold my hand along the way, I never would have even begun this book. His friendship and love have been the fuel to keep me going.

Another special thank you goes to my children, Michael and Katie, as well as the rest of my family including my brothers and in-laws. Everyone's advice and ideas are entwined in all the stories, dialogues, and pictures throughout this book. I appreciate as well all my colleagues and friends and my sister-in-law, Denise Baker, who participated in proofreading and editing. An extra special thanks goes to Pam McDonald for her original drawings and illustrations, and the many hours spent helping the ideas take life!

I'd also like to thank AFS for accepting me, many years ago, to participate in the program. The people I met through AFS and the experiences I had as an exchange student changed the path of my life forever.

Lastly, I'd like to thank all the students who have taken my class. Their gratitude and curiosity inspired me to write this book. Although I don't have teacher's pets in my classes, I must admit that one will always remain a favorite: Steve Hickner, who out of sheer kindness and enthusiasm for learning, transformed the original illustrations into true art! I am forever truly grateful for his talent, generosity, and dedication to lifelong learning!

What Can We Learn Today?

Chapter	Chapter Title	Page
1	Where Were We? Review of Level One Basic Material	1
2	The Here and Now Review of Verbs in Present Tense	5
3	What Was That Again? Review of Verbs in Simple Past Tenses	18
4	What's "It" to Ya? Direct and Indirect Object Pronouns	37
5	Mirror Mirror on the Wall, Here's the Fairest Pronoun of Them All Reflexive Verbs	58
6	Let's Get It Done! Commands and Pronouns	69
7	Are You in the Mood? Present Subjunctive	85
8	Were You in the Mood? Past Subjunctive	102
9	What Have You Done? Present Perfect	113
10	What We Had Done Pluperfect	123
11	What's in The Crystal Ball? The Future Tense	129
12	What WOULD You Do? The Conditional Tense	137
13	Look What You Can Do! Mastery Exercises	144
	Cheat Sheets Appendix	151

Chapter 1
Where Were We?
Review of Level One Material

Read the following dialogues with your partner. Remember, as you read these aloud, try to understand the overall meaning of the whole conversation. Don't worry if you don't know some words – try to put the pieces together to understand the overall meaning. Check your understanding with the English translation in the appendix of this book.

Diálogo 1.1
Read this conversation between two people who are meeting each other for the first time. Then, answer the questions that follow.

Personaje A - Buenos días, Señora.

Personaje B - Hola. ¿Cómo está Ud.?

Personaje A – Estoy muy bien, gracias. ¿Cómo se llama Ud.?

Personaje B – Me llamo Alicia González. ¿Y Ud.?

Personaje A – Mucho gusto, Alicia. Me llamo Sofía Lorén.

Personaje B - ¿Sofía Lorén? Pero Ud. no es la modelo famosa, ¿verdad?

Personaje A - Claro que no, Alicia. No soy modelo. Estoy jubilada ahora, pero yo era

contadora. También soy su nueva vecina. Compramos esta casa en junio.

Antes, vivíamos en Miami.

Personaje B – Bueno, mucho gusto, Sofía. Y bienvenida a la vecindad.

Preguntas:

1. ¿Son los personajes del diálogo hombres o mujeres?

2. ¿Dónde están? ¿En una calle cerca de la casa de Sofía o en un supermercado?

3. ¿Qué hora es? ¿Son las dos de la tarde o son las diez de la mañana?

4. ¿Cuál es la profesión de Sofía ahora?

5. ¿Dónde vivía Sofía antes de comprar la casa nueva en junio?

Diálogo 1.2

Read this conversation between two students in class. Answer the questions that follow.

Tomás –   Hola, amigo. ¿Qué tal?

Francisco -   Regular, gracias. ¿Y tú?

Tomás –   Estoy bien. Me llamo Tomás. ¿Y tú? ¿Cómo te llamas?

Francisco –   Me llamo Francisco. Hace seis semanas que estudio español y yo no comprendo mucho.

Tomás –   Es un placer, Francisco. ¡Tú hablas muy bien el español! ¿De dónde eres tú?

Francisco –   Yo soy de Europa – de Alemania. ¿Y tú?

Tomás -   Soy de Colombia – de Bogotá. Pero ahora vivo aquí en Glendale, California. Me gusta mucho California. Siempre hace buen tiempo y las playas son muy bonitas.

Francisco -   Estoy de acuerdo. Bueno, Francisco, ¿qué te gusta hacer en tu tiempo libre? ¿Tienes unos pasatiempos favoritos?

Tomás –   A ver… me gusta mucho viajar. También me gusta leer novelas de misterio y pasar tiempo con mi familia y amigos.

Francisco –   A mí me encanta viajar y pasar tiempo con mi familia. Me gusta escuchar música y mirar películas en el cine.

Tomás -   ¿Te gustan los deportes?

Francisco –   No, no me gustan los deportes. Pero, me gusta el arte. Y, ¿a ti te gusta el arte también?

Tomás -   Sí, más o menos… no tanto. A mi mejor amigo le encanta el arte.

Francisco –   Bueno, Tomás. Fue un placer. Tengo que ir a mi casa. Nos vemos.

Tomás –   Hasta la próxima.

Preguntas

1. ¿Cuánto tiempo hace que Francisco estudia el español?
2. ¿Comprende mucho o poco español Francisco?
3. ¿De dónde es Tomás?
4. ¿Dónde viven Tomás y Francisco ahora?
5. A Francisco ¿qué le gusta hacer en su tiempo libre?
6. ¿Qué les gusta hacer mucho a Tomás y a Francisco?
7. ¿A Tomás y a Francisco les gustan los deportes?
8. ¿A quién le gusta leer novelas?
9. ¿A quién no le gusta mucho el arte?
10. ¿Adónde va Francisco?

Práctica 1.1

Now it's your turn! Read through the conversation from "Diálogo 1.2" again with your partner. This time, replace all bold, italicized parts with real information about yourselves.

Estudiante A – Hola, **amigo**. ¿Qué tal?

Estudiante B - **Regular**, gracias. ¿Y tú?

Estudiante A - **Estoy bien**. Me llamo **Tomás**. ¿Y tú? ¿Cómo te llamas?

Estudiante B - Me llamo **Francisco**. Hace **seis semanas** que estudio español y yo **no comprendo** mucho.

Estudiante A - Es un placer, **Francisco**. ¡Tú hablas muy bien el español! ¿De dónde eres tú?

Estudiante B - Yo soy de **Europa – de Alemania**. ¿Y tú?

Estudiante A - Soy de **Colombia – de Bogotá**. Pero ahora vivo aquí en **Glendale, California**. **Me gusta** mucho California. **Siempre hace buen tiempo y las playas son muy bonitas.**

Estudiante B - **Estoy de acuerdo**. Bueno, **Francisco**, ¿qué te gusta hacer en tu tiempo libre? ¿Tienes unos pasatiempos favoritos?

Estudiante A – A ver… me gusta mucho **viajar**. También me gusta **leer novelas de misterio y pasar tiempo con mi familia y amigos.**

Estudiante B - A mí me **encanta viajar y pasar tiempo con mi familia**. Me gusta **escuchar música y mirar películas en el cine.**

Estudiante A - ¿Te gustan **los deportes**?

Estudiante B - **No, no me gustan los deportes**. Pero, me gusta **el arte**. Y, ¿a ti te gusta **el arte** también?

Estudiante A - **Sí, más o menos… no tanto. A mi mejor amigo** le encanta **el arte**.

Estudiante B - Bueno, **Tomás**. Fue un placer. Tengo que **ir a mi casa**. Nos vemos.

Estudiante A – Hasta la próxima.

Preguntas:
1. ¿Cómo se llama tu compañero(a)?
2. ¿De dónde es él/ella?
3. A tu compañero(a), ¿qué le gusta hacer en su tiempo libre?
4. ¿A tu compañero(a) le gustan o no le gustan las mismas actividades que a ti te gustan?
5. ¿Quién tiene que ir? ¿Tú o tu compañero(a)? ¿Adónde va/vas?

Práctica 1.2

Study the picture below. Then, discuss with your partner your answers to the questions that follow.

1. ¿Dónde están las personas en este dibujo? ¿Están en la casa, la biblioteca, o en la clase?
2. ¿Quién es la mujer con los anteojos? ¿Es vendedora, directora, maestra o bibliotecaria?
3. ¿De qué hablan las personas? ¿Hablan de una composición, un examen, o de todas las notas en una clase?
4. ¿Tiene el chico buenas o malas notas?
5. Al chico, ¿qué deporte le gusta más? ¿Le gusta el fútbol o el béisbol?
6. ¿Está preocupado o está tranquilo el chico?
7. ¿Está contenta o preocupada la mamá del chico?
8. ¿Qué hace la maestra... le explica las notas o habla de los goles del partido de fútbol?

Chapter 2
The Here and Now
Review of Verbs in Present Tense

Repaso Gramatical – los verbos en el tiempo presente

❖ Remember that verbs in a sentence generally need to be conjugated to match the subject of the sentence.

Ejemplos:

1. trabajar	To work	Yo trabajo en una oficina	I work in an office.
2. comprender	To comprehend	Tú y yo comprendemos el español muy bien.	You and I (we) understand Spanish well.
3. abrir	To open	¿Abrió Ud. la puerta?	Did you open the door?

In Level 1, you learned the present, preterite, and imperfect tenses.

Ejemplos:

1. **Present Tense**	Ella estudia español.	She studies (is studying) Spanish.
2. **Preterite Tense**	Ella estudió español por dos años.	She studied Spanish for two years.
3. **Imperfect Tense**	Ella estudiaba español en Madrid.	She used to study (was studying) Spanish in Madrid.

Here is a quick review of the how to form the present tense conjugations.

Drop the –AR, -ER, or –Ir from the infinitive and add the following endings:

-AR		- ER		-IR	
Yo **- o**	Nosotros(as) **-amos**	Yo **- o**	Nosotros(as) **-emos**	Yo **- o**	Nosotros(as) **-imos**
Tú **-as**	Vosotros(as) **-áis**	Tú **-es**	Vosotros(as) **-éis**	Tú **-es**	Vosotros(as) **-ís**
Ud. Él **-a** Ella	Uds. Ellos **-an** Ellas	Ud. Él **-e** Ella	Uds. Ellos **-en** Ellas	Ud. Él **-e** Ella	Uds. Ellos **-en** Ellas

Práctica 2.1

Conjugate these verbs to the present tense to create verb phrases that match the subject provided.

1. bailar (to dance)	They dance	
2. vender (to sell)	I am selling	
3. subir (to climb, go up)	He climbs	
4. esperar (to wait)	You (my friend) wait	
5. leer (to read)	We read (are reading)	
6. recibir (to receive)	You guys receive	
7. viajar (to travel)	We travel	
8. llegar (to arrive)	You all arrive	
9. aprender (to learn)	I am learning	
10. creer (to believe)	They believe	
11. comer (to eat)	We are eating	
12. vivir (to live)	You (my friend) live	
13. trabajar (to work)	She works	
14. cantar (to sing)	You (my friend) sing	
15. recibir (to receive)	They receive	
16. necesitar (to need)	I need	

Práctica 2.2

Study the following scene. Then, discuss with your partner the answers to the questions that follow.

1. ¿Dónde están las personas? ¿Están en el aeropuerto o en el hotel?
2. ¿Qué hace la mujer en el sillón? ¿Crees que espera a otra persona o descansa?
3. ¿Necesita la mujer en el mostrador la cuenta o un cuarto? ¿Qué hay en el sobre (the envelope)?
4. ¿Está enojado el hombre con la maleta porque espera en la cola o porque necesita ayuda con su maleta?
5. ¿Llega o sale el hombre con la maleta?
6. ¿Necesita un cuarto el hombre con la maleta?
7. ¿Quién es el hombre alto con el sombrero? ¿Es cliente o empleado del hotel?
8. ¿Qué mira el hombre con la maleta? ¿Mira su reloj o su teléfono?
9. ¿Es un hotel moderno o tradicional?
10. ¿Ocurre esta escena en un cuarto del hotel o en el vestíbulo del hotel?

There were many irregular verbs in the present tense. Here are some that you learned:

1. Irregular "yo"

2. Stem-changing or "Shoe Verbs" ("e" to "ie", "o" to "ue", and "e" to "I"

3. Completely Irregular

Irregular "yo" (with all other forms working just like the regular verbs)

Verb	"Yo" Form	Verb	"Yo" Form
Agradecer (to thank)	agradezco	Reconocer (to recognize)	reconozco
Conocer (to know a person, be familiar with)	conozco	Saber (to know a fact, how to do something)	sé
Dar (to give)	doy	Salir (to leave, go out)	salgo
Hacer (to do, to make)	hago	Traducir (to translate)	traduzco
Ofrecer (to offer)	ofrezco	Traer (to bring)	traigo
Poner (to put, place)	pongo	Ver (to see)	veo

Práctica 2.3

Read each sentence and decide if it is true or false about yourself. Write "C" if the statement is true (cierto) or "F" if the statement is false (falso). Then, turn the statement into a question and ask your partner if these situations are true or false about him/herself as well. (To change the first statement to a question, you would ask "¿Sales mucho con tus amigos los fines de semana?")

Frase	Cierto/Falso para mí	Cierto/Falso para mi compañero(a)
1. Salgo mucho con mis amigos los fines de semana.		
2. Conozco bien a una persona famosa.		

3. Reconozco fácilmente a las personas.		
4. Sé tocar un instrumento.		
5. Hago ejercicio todos los días.		
6. Les doy regalos a mis amigos de vez en cuando.		
7. Pongo mis llaves en el mismo lugar cada vez que entro en mi casa.		
8. Traigo comida o bebidas a las fiestas.		

❖ Some verbs have a spelling change in the stem of the verb. There is no way to know that a verb has this type of irregularity except to memorize them. Memorizing is easier with lots of practice. To practice with these verbs, try picking a few verbs a day to use in sentences.

These verbs have three possible stem changes:

1. e → ie	2. o → ue	3. e → i
pensar – to think	dormir – to sleep	repetir – to repeat

pienso	pensamos	duermo	dormimos	repito	repetimos
piensas	pensáis	duermes	dormís	repites	repetís
piensa	piensan	duerme	duermen	repite	repiten

Stem-Changing Verbs "e" to "ie"

Calentar	To heat
Cerrar	To close
Comenzar	To begin
Confesar	To confess
Defender	To defend

Despertar(se)	To wake up
Divertir(se)	To enjoy (oneself)/ to have fun
Empezar	To start
Encender	To light/ignite
Entender	To understand
Hervir	To boil
Mentir	To lie (not tell the truth)
Merendar	To have a snack
Negar	To deny
Nevar	To snow
Pensar	To think
Perder	To lose
Preferir	To prefer
Querer	To want
Sentar(se)	To sit down
Sentir(se)	To feel, to regret, to be sorry

Práctica 2.4

Change the verb to match the subject. Then, translate the sentences to English.

1. Mi mamá _____ (hervir) el agua para hacer té.

2. Uds. _____ (preferir) ir al restaurante chino, ¿no?

3. ¿Quiénes _____ (despertarse) temprano por las mañanas?

4. Yo no _____ (entender) la pregunta.

5. Mi familia _____ (querer) pasar dos semanas en España.

6. Yo no _____ (perder) muchas cosas.

7. _____ (Nevar) mucho en las montañas.

8. El policía siempre _____ (defender) a la gente.

Práctica 2.5

Look at the following picture and discuss the answers to the questions with your partner.

1. ¿En qué piensa la mujer? ¿Piensa en mirar una película o en tomar un crucero?
2. ¿Prefiere el hombre tomar un crucero o mirar la televisión en casa?
3. ¿Empieza o termina la cita? ¿Cómo sabes?
4. ¿ Meriendan o cenan las personas?
5. ¿Se divierten los dos? ¿Cómo sabes?

Stem-Changing Verbs "o" to "ue"

Acostar(se)	To lie down/go to bed
Almorzar	To eat/have lunch
Colgar	To hang
Contar	To count, to tell (a story, a joke, etc.)
Costar	To cost
Descolgar	To unhook/unhang

11

Devolver	To return (an item)
Dormir	To sleep
Encontrar	To find
Llover	To rain
Morir	To die
Mostrar	To show
Mover	To move (some item)
Oler	To smell (huelo, hueles, huele, olemos, oléis, huelen)
Poder	To be able to, can
Recordar	To remember
Soñar (con)	To dream (about)
Tronar	To thunder
Volar	To fly
Volver	To return, come back

Práctica 2.6

Answer the following questions about yourself in column two. Then, ask your partner the same questions. See how many answers you have in common. For each answer that matches yours, make a check mark in the final column.

Pregunta	Mi respuesta	¡Tenemos la misma respuesta!
1. ¿Te acuestas antes o después de las once de la noche?	*Me acuesto...*	
2. Generalmente, ¿almuerzas en casa o en un restaurante?		
3. ¿Cuentas chistes (jokes) buenos?		
4. ¿Recuerdas mejor los nombres o las caras (faces) de las personas?		

5. ¿Puedes hacer algo (something) interesante? ¿Qué es?		

Stem-Changing "e" to "i"

Competir	To compete
Despedir(se) de	To say goodbye to
Medir	To measure
Pedir	To ask for, order
Reír(se) (de) (río, ríes, ríe, reímos, reís, ríen)	To laugh (at)
Repetir	To repeat
Seguir (sigo, sigues, sigue, seguimos, seguís, siguen)	To continue, to follow
Servir	To serve
Sonreír(se)	To smile
Vestir(se)	To get dressed

Práctica 2.7

Translate the following questions to Spanish. Then, write your answer to the question in Spanish in the space provided. Afterwards, ask your partner for his/her answers.

1. Do you compete in any sports?

_____

2. What flavor (sabor) do you order in an ice cream shop (una heladería)?

_____

3. What do you laugh at?

_____

4. Who serves the meals in your house?

_____

5. Do you follow the rules (las reglas)?

_____

6. Do you measure two times and cut (cortar) once?

_____

❖ Some verbs are completely irregular, meaning they do not follow any regular pattern. Again, memorizing these conjugations is easier if you use the verbs often in your conversations.

Completely Irregular Verbs in the Present Tense

Verb	Yo	Tú	Ud., Él, Ella	Nosotros	Vosotros	Uds., Ellos, Ellas
Ser (to be) Description, Occupation, Characteristic, Time/Date, Origin, Relationship (DOCTOR)	Soy	Eres	Es	Somos	Sois	Son
Estar (to be) Position, Location, Action, Condition, Emotion (PLACE)	Estoy	Estás	Está	Estamos	Estáis	Están
Ir (to go)	Voy	Vas	Va	Vamos	Vais	Van
Decir (to say, tell)	Digo	Dices	Dice	Decimos	Decís	Dicen
Tener (to have)	Tengo	Tienes	Tiene	Tenemos	Tenéis	Tienen
Oír (to hear)	Oigo	Oyes	Oye	Oímos	Oís	Oyen
Venir (to come)	Vengo	Vienes	Viene	Venimos	Venís	Vienen

Práctica 2.8

Read the following story and answer the questions that follow.

Aquí tengo una foto de mi amiga, Carolina. Ella es la dueña de una tienda de ropa atlética. Su tienda está en el centro de la ciudad. Es una tienda pequeña pero tiene mucha ropa muy bonita con precios razonables. Carolina vive aquí en los Estados Unidos, pero es originalmente de Chile. En la foto, Carolina está enfrente de su casa, pero ahora, ella está en Santiago, Chile porque está visitando a su familia – a sus tíos y primos que viven allí. Ella va a volver en dos semanas. Su prima, Victoria viene con ella para visitar a los Estados Unidos por primera vez. Oigo de Carolina que su prima es muy simpática y muy buena gente. Carolina siempre dice que su prima Victoria es su prima favorita.

1. ¿Está el narrador con Carolina en este momento?
2. ¿Cuál es la profesión de Carolina?
3. ¿Qué tipo de ropa vende en la tienda de Carolina?
4. ¿Qué oye el narrador sobre la prima de Carolina?
5. ¿Cuándo van a llegar Carolina y Victoria a los Estados Unidos?

❖ Remember that the verb "tener" is used to form many expressions where "tener" does not translate directly to "to have"

Tener frío	To be cold
Tener calor	To be hot
Tener sed	To be thirsty
Tener hambre	To be hungry
Tener vergüenza (de)	To be ashamed (of)
Tener suerte	To be lucky
Tener prisa	To be in a hurry
Tener cuidado	To be careful
Tener miedo (de)	To be afraid (of)
Tener sueño	To be sleepy
Tener (#) años	To be (#) years old
Tener éxito	To be successful
Tener lugar	To take place
Tener que ver con	To have to do with
Tener ganas de + infinitive	To feel like doing something
Tener que + infinitive	To have to do something

Práctica 2.9

Discuss the following questions with your partner. Compare your answers.

1. ¿De qué tienes miedo?
2. ¿Crees que unas personas tienen suerte y otras no? ¿Por qué?
3. ¿Tienes sueño todos los días? ¿Con qué frecuencia tienes sueño?
4. ¿Generalmente tienes hambre por las mañanas?
5. ¿Cuántos años debe tener una persona para tomar alcohol?
6. ¿Cuántos años debe tener una persona para casarse?
7. ¿Cómo sabes que una persona tiene éxito? ¿Cuándo tiene éxito una persona? ¿Tienes éxito? ¿Por qué?
8. Después de comer helado, ¿tienes sed?

Práctica 2.10

Identify who is being described. Use the pictures on the next page to see who is being described.

1. ¿Quién tiene sed?

2. ¿Quién tiene ganas de nadar?

3. ¿Quién tiene éxito?

4. ¿Quién tiene vergüenza?

5. ¿Quién tiene hambre?

6. ¿Quién tiene mucha suerte?

7. ¿Quién tiene que hacer la cama?

8. ¿Quién tiene frío?

Juan

Tomás

Patricia

Miguel

Susana

Carlitos

Mamá

Emilio

Dorotea

17

Chapter 3
What Was That Again?
Review of Verbs in Simple Past Tenses

❖ There are two simple past tenses in Spanish – the Preterite and the Imperfect
❖ The preterite tense is used to express a completed action in the past (the speaker knows when the action began and ended)
❖ The imperfect tense is used to describe, to paint a picture, or to tell about a past event where the speaker doesn't know, or doesn't want to emphasize, when the action either began or ended.

Comparison of the uses of Preterite vs. the Imperfect Tense

Preterite	Imperfect
1. Completed or finished one-time actions in the past *Ejemplo: Yo cerré la puerta. (I closed the door.)*	1. Ongoing or continuous actions *Ejemplo: Estudiaba la literatura en la universidad. (I studied/used to study Literature in the university.)*
2. Actions that took place for a specific number of times *Ejemplo: Visité a mi abuela cinco veces el mes pasado. (I visited my grandmother five times last month.)*	2. Repeated or habitual actions *Ejemplo: Mi familia siempre iba a la playa durante los veranos. (My family always used to go/went to the beach during the summers.)*
3. Actions that took place during an enclosed period of time *Ejemplo: Pasé una semana en Francia. (I spent one week in France.)*	3. Descriptions *Ejemplo: Cuando era niño, mi hermano era mi bajo y tenía los ojos avellanos. (When he was a little boy, my brother was short and had hazel eyes.)*
	4. Time or date and age *Ejemplo: Eran las tres cuando salimos. (It was 3:00 when we left.)* *Ejemplo: Yo tenía tres años ella se murió. (I was three years old when she died.)*
	5. Description of an event that was in progress when another event occurred. *Ejemplo: Los estudiantes leían cuando la profesora entró. (The students were reading when the teacher entered.)*
	6. Mental activities or emotions *Ejemplo: Yo siempre quería ser maestra. (I always wanted to be a teacher.)*

Práctica 3.1

Decide if the italicized verb in the sentence would be in the preterite or imperfect based on the context of the sentence. Then write the number of the rule that is being used.

1. My mom *gave* me a book for my birthday last year.
2. We *used to go* to my cousins' house every weekend.
3. I *studied* French for three years.
4. He *was talking* on the phone when I arrived.
5. He was talking on the phone when I *arrived*.
6. How many times *did you see* that movie?
7. It *was* 5:00 when the President addressed the nation.
8. I *read* that book three times.
9. She *was* ten years old when he last visited.
10. Who *brought* the salad?

1. P or I   Rule # ____
2. P or I   Rule # ____
3. P or I   Rule # ____
4. P or I   Rule # ____
5. P or I   Rule # ____
6. P or I   Rule # ____
7. P or I   Rule # ____
8. P or I   Rule # ____
9. P or I   Rule # ____
10. P or I   Rule # ____

❖ To form the Imperfect Tense, drop off the final ending –AR, -ER, or –IR of the verb infinitive, and add the following endings:

For – AR verbs:

Yo	Nosotros
- aba	**- ábamos**
Tú	Vosotros
- abas	**- abais**
Ud., él, ella	Uds., ellos, ellas
- aba	**- aban**

For – ER and –IR Verbs:

Yo	Nosotros
- ía	**- íamos**
Tú	Vosotros
- ía	**- íais**
Ud., él, ella	Uds., ellos, ellas
- ía	**- ían**

❖ There are three irregular verbs:

ser – to be

Era	Éramos
Eras	Erais
Era	Eran

ir – to go

Iba	Íbamos
Ibas	Ibais
Iba	Iban

ver – to see

Veía	Veíamos
Veías	Veíais
Veía	Veían

19

Diálogo 3.1

Read the following dialogue between two people who want to get to know more about the other person's past. See if you can understand the meaning of the Imperfect verbs in the sentences.

Tomás:	Alisa, ¿cómo **eras** cuando **tenías** ocho años? ¿**Eras** obediente o desobediente?
Alisa:	Yo **era** muy obediente. Siempre **escuchaba** a mis padres y **seguía** todas las reglas.
Tomás:	No lo dudo. Eres una ángel todavía.
Alisa:	Ay, Tomás... eres muy amable. ¿Y tú? ¿Cómo **eras** de niño?
Tomás:	No lo quieres saber. Yo **era** muy desobediente. Siempre me **peleaba** con mis hermanos. Y nunca **ayudaba** en casa. **Era** muy perezoso. Pero, siempre **sacaba** buenas notas en la escuela porque **era** muy inteligente y diligente con mi tarea.
Alisa:	¿Qué más? ¿Qué **hacías** con tus amigos? ¿**Tenías** muchos amigos?
Tomás:	Sí, sí, **tenía** amigos, pero no muchos. Sólo los niños que **vivían** cerca de mi casa. Nosotros **andábamos** en bicicleta o **jugábamos** a los videojuegos. A veces **íbamos** al parque para jugar al baloncesto. Nos **gustaba** mucho pasar todo el día afuera, jugando a los deportes.

Práctica 3.2

Answer the following questions about the dialogue.

1. ¿Cómo era Alisa de niña? ¿Obediente o desobediente? ¿Y Tomás?

2. ¿Es Alisa diferente o la misma de cuando era niña?

3. ¿Por qué dice Tomás que él era perezoso?

4. ¿Adónde iban Tomás y sus amigos para jugar a los deportes?

Práctica 3.3

Now describe yourself when you were little. Write your answer on the space provided. Then, ask your partner the same questions.

1. Cuando eras niño(a), ¿eras tú obediente o desobediente?

_____

2. Cuando eras niño(a), ¿tocabas un instrumento? ¿Qué instrumento?

_____

3. ¿Dónde vivías?

_____

4. Cuando eras niño(a), ¿practicabas un deporte? ¿Qué deporte?

_____

5. ¿Ibas de vacaciones todos los veranos? ¿Adónde ibas generalmente?

_____

Práctica 3.4

*Read the following story about my grandmother. Then, change all the bold, italicized words to personalize the story for you. Talk about someone **you** know/knew and find/found interesting. Read the information to your partner. Use this bank of words to help you. If a sentence or idea doesn't apply to you, just leave it out or replace it with something else.*

Cariñoso(a) = caring, affectionate	Sonreírse = to smile	Lo/la = him/her	Lejos de = far from
Cerca de = near	Cuidar a = to take care of	Ganarse la vida = to earn a living	La mascota = the pet
Un pájaro = a bird	Un pez = a (live) fish	Un gato = a cat	Un perro = a dog
Abuelo = grandfather	Primo(a) = cousin	Tío(a) = uncle/aunt	Hermano(a) = brother/sister

Mi abuela era una persona muy especial para mí. *Mi abuela* se llamaba *Clara*, y *ella* era muy *amable* y *cariñosa*. Siempre se *sonreía* cuando yo *la* visitaba. *Ella* vivía en *Glendale, California*, muy *cerca* de la casa de mi familia. *Ella* era de *Alemania* originalmente. Mi *abuela cuidaba a los niños de la vecindad*. Se ganaba la vida así. *Ella* pasaba mucho tiempo en *la casa*. *Limpiaba* mucho y *su casa siempre estaba perfecta*. *Cocinaba* bien, y le gustaba *jugar los juegos con los niños*. También le gustaba *escuchar música del piano.* Le gustaban *los animales* y tenía una mascota. Ella tenía *un pájaro que*

siempre estaba en su jaula en la cocina de su casa. El pájaro se llamaba *Timmy.*

Muchas veces *mi abuela* y *yo le bañábamos a Timmy. Mi abuela* amaba mucho a *su*

esposo, mi abuelo. Pero mi abuelo se murió cuando ellos tenían cincuenta y nueve años.

Mi abuela vivía sola después de la muerte de mi abuelo. Pero siempre estaba *contenta*

porque era *optimista*, y así vivía una vida muy *feliz.*

❖ To form the Preterite Tense, drop off the final ending –AR, -ER, or –IR of the verb infinitive, and add the following endings:

For – AR verbs:

Yo **- é**	Nosotros **- amos**
Tú **- aste**	Vosotros **- asteis**
Ud., él, ella **- ó**	Uds., ellos, ellas **- aron**

For – ER and –IR Verbs:

Yo **- í**	Nosotros **- imos**
Tú **- iste**	Vosotros **- isteis**
Ud., él, ella **- ió**	Uds., ellos, ellas **- ieron**

Práctica 3.5

See how much you and your partner have in common. Read the statement in column one, and in column two, state whether it's true or false about yourself. In column three, change the verb from the infinitive to its appropriate preterite conjugation for "tú" so you can ask your partner if he/she did that activity in the past. Then, ask your partner if he/she did the activity mentioned and in column four, write his/her response.

Actividad del pasado	¿Cierto o falso sobre mí?	Verbo conjugado en el pretérito en la forma "tú"	¿Cierto o falso sobre mi compañero(a)?
1. Viajé a España.			
2. Comí una comida exótica una vez.			

3. Viví en otro país por más de un año.			
4. Escribí una autobiografía.			
5. Vendí algo que yo no quería vender.			
6. Miré una película anoche.			
7. Perdí una cosa importante recientemente.			
8. Trabajé hasta muy tarde anoche.			
9. Dormí por menos de 7 horas anoche.			
10. Canté en la ducha esta mañana.			
11. Leí muchos libros el año pasado.			
12. Estudié el español anoche.			
13. Compré algo muy caro e innecesario una vez.			
14. Participé en un deporte en la escuela secundaria.			
15. Tomé café esta mañana.			
16. Escuché música buena en un concierto recientemente.			
17. Limpié mi casa este fin de semana pasado.			
18. Me acosté tarde anoche.			
19. Conocí a mi mejor amigo(a) en una clase en la escuela primaria.			
20. Leí un libro entero más de dos veces.			
21. Viví en un lugar por más de diez años.			
22. Recibí una multa (ticket) este año.			
23. Recibí buenas notas (grades) en la escuela secundaria.			
24. Me levanté temprano esta mañana.			
25. Me mudé muchas veces durante mi juventud.			

- ❖ There are MANY irregular verbs in the preterite tense. The irregularities generally fall within one of these groupings:
  1. Spell-changing verbs (-CAR, -GAR, -ZAR verbs)
  2. Stem-changing -IR Verbs
  3. "I" to "Y" Verbs
  4. 18 Irregulars (which includes the "U" group, the "I" group, and the "J" group)

Spell-changing verbs (-CAR, -GAR, -ZAR verbs)

These verbs have a spelling change in the "yo" form so the pronunciation of the conjugated verb remains consistent with the infinitive sound.

- ❖ Verbs ending with -CAR: in the "yo" form, the "cé" changes to "qué"
- ❖ Verbs ending with -GAR: in the "yo" form, the "gé" changes to "gué"
- ❖ Verbs ending with -ZAR: in the "yo" form, the "zé" changes to "cé"

Ejemplos:

buscar – to look for		llegar – to arrive		cruzar – to cross	
bus**qué**	buscamos	lle**gué**	llegamos	cru**cé**	cruzamos
buscaste	buscasteis	llegaste	llegasteis	cruzaste	cruzasteis
buscó	buscaron	llegó	llegaron	cruzó	cruzaron

Los verbos -CAR		Los verbos -GAR		Los verbos -ZAR	
Buscar	To look for	Cargar	to load, carry	Abrazar	To hug
Equivocar(se)	To be mistaken	Entregar	to hand over, deliver	Comenzar	To begin
Explicar	To explain	Jugar	To play (a game, sport)	Cruzar	To cross
Sacar	To take out	Llegar	To arrive	Empezar	To start
Tocar	To play (an instrument)	Pagar	To pay	Gozar	To enjoy

Práctica 3.6

Complete the sentence with the preterite tense of the most logical verb from the list of -CAR, -GAR, -ZAR verbs.

1. Yo _____ la guitarra anoche.

2. Yo le _____ la tarea a la maestra.

24

3. ¿Les _____ la maestra la lección a los estudiantes hoy?

4. Yo _____ al tenis ayer por la tarde.

5. ¿_____ tú tarde a la clase anoche?

6. Yo _____ mi pluma de mi mochila al llegar a la clase.

7. Mi esposo y yo _____ la cuenta y salimos del restaurante.

8. ¿_____ Uds. la calle para llegar al cine?

9. El programa _____ a las ocho de la noche.

10. Mi información no es correcta. Yo _____.

Stem Changing –IR Verbs

All –IR verbs that were stem changing verbs in the present tense have a stem change in the preterite as well.

- ❖ The stem change only occurs in the third person singular and plural (él, ella, Ud., ellos, ellas, Uds.)
- ❖ The stem changes from "e" to "i" or "o" to "u"

Ejemplos:

pedir – to ask for, order   **reír – to laugh**   **dormir – to sleep**

Pedí	Pedimos		Reí	Reímos		Dormí	Dormimos
Pediste	Pedisteis		Reíste	Reísteis		Dormiste	Dormisteis
Pidió	Pidieron		Rió	Rieron		DUrmió	dUrmieron

Stem changing –IR Verbs

Competir	To compete
Despedir(se) de	To say goodbye to
Divertir(se)	To have fun, to enjoy oneself
Dormir	To sleep
Hervir	To boil
Medir	To measure
Mentir	To lie
Morir	To die

Pedir	To ask for, order
Preferir	To prefer
Reír	To laugh
Repetir	To repeat
Seguir	To follow, continue
Servir	To serve
Sonreír	To smile
Sentir(se)	To feel, to regret, to be sorry
Vestir(se)	To get dressed

Práctica 3.7
Translate the following sentences.

1. My kids/children slept for few hours last night.

   _____

2. ¿Did your friends say goodbye to you? (Note: after a preposition, use "mí" or "ti" for "me" and "you")

   ¿_____?

3. I laughed when I heard the joke. (the joke = el chiste)

   _____

4. Mr. and Mrs. Molina, did you both prefer the book or the movie?

   ¿ _____

   _____?

5. Did he regret his decision?

   ¿ _____?

6. They didn't lie; they enjoyed themselves a lot.

   _____

   _____

7. What did you all order?

_____

8. The teacher repeated the new words.

_____

"I" to "Y" Verbs

These verbs have a spelling change in the third person singular and plural forms (the Ud, él, ella, Uds., ellos and ellas forms)

❖ These verbs have a vowel preceding the ending of the infinitive

Ejemplos:

oír – to hear			leer – to read			caer(se) – fall down			creer – to believe	
Oí	Oímos		Leí	Leímos		Me caí	Nos Caímos		Creí	Creímos
Oíste	Oísteis		Leíste	Leísteis		Te caíste	Os caísteis		Creíste	Creísteis
Oyó	oyeron		leyó	leyeron		Se cayó	Se cayeron		Creyó	Creyeron

Práctica 3.8

Translate the following sentences.

1. He believed the story. (the story = la historia)

_____

2. Did you all hear the news? (the news = las noticias)

¿ _____ ?

3. Who fell down?

¿ _____ ?

4. Did he read the article today?

¿ _____ ?

Completely Irregular Verbs

There are several completely irregular verbs. There is a bit of a pattern, however with these verbs.

❖ If you learn the first person singular form of the verb, the other forms are all very similar.

❖ Many of these verbs fit into one of the following groups based upon their stem: The "I" group, the "U" group, and the "J" group. The words have been separated into those categories below.

"I" Group

Verb	English	Yo	Tú	Ud., él, ella	Nosotros	Vosotros	Uds., ellos, ellas
Dar	To give	Di	Diste	Dio	Dimos	Disteis	Dieron
Hacer	To do, to make	Hice	Hiciste	Hizo	Hicimos	Hicisteis	Hicieron
Ir	To go	Fui	Fuiste	Fue	Fuimos	Fuisteis	Fueron
Querer	To want	Quise	Quisiste	Quiso	Quisimos	Quisisteis	Quisieron
Ser	To be (DOCTOR)	Fui	Fuiste	Fue	Fuimos	Fuisteis	Fueron
Venir	To come	Vine	Viniste	Vino	Vinimos	Vinisteis	Vinieron
Ver	To see	Vi	Viste	Vio	Vimos	Visteis	Vieron

"U" Group

Verb	English	Yo	Tú	Ud., él, ella	Nosotros	Vosotros	Uds., ellos, ellas
Andar	To walk	Anduve	Anduviste	Anduvo	Anduvimos	Anduvisteis	Anduvieron
Estar	To be (PLACE)	Estuve	Estuviste	Estuvo	Estuvimos	Estuvisteis	Estuvieron
Poder	To be able to, to manage	Pude	Pudiste	Pudo	Pudimos	Pudisteis	Pudieron
Poner	To put, to place	Puse	Pusiste	Puso	Pusimos	Pusisteis	Pusieron
Saber	To find out (in preterite, "saber" changes meaning	Supe	Supiste	Supo	Supimos	Supisteis	Supieron
Tener	To have	Tuve	Tuviste	Tuvo	Tuvimos	Tuvisteis	Tuvieron

"J" Group

Verb	English	Yo	Tú	Ud., él, ella	Nosotros	Vosotros	Uds., ellos, ellas
Conducir	To drive, conduct	Conduje	Condujiste	Condujo	Condujimos	Condujisteis	Condujeron
Decir	To say, to tell	Dije	Dijiste	Dijo	Dijimos	Dijisteis	Dijeron
Traducir	To translate	Traduje	Tradujiste	Tradujo	Tradujimos	Tradujisteis	Tradujeron
Traer	To bring	Traje	Trajiste	Trajo	Trajimos	Trajisteis	Trajeron

Práctica 3.9

Translate the following questions. Then, ask your partner the questions and discuss your answers. **Note:** *"Ningún" and "Ninguna" mean "not any" or "not one".*

1. Did you bring a pen to the class tonight?

¿_____?

2. Did you drive to an interesting place today? (a place = un lugar)

¿_____?

3. What did you make for dinner tonight? (The dinner = la cena)

¿_____?

4. Were you able to sleep well last night?

¿_____?

5. Where were you yesterday?

¿_____?

6. How you find out about this class?

¿_____?

Práctica 3.10

Choose one partner to read the story and ask the questions in parenthesis. The other partner will listen and answer the questions. Remember, if you need help, the answers will be in the appendix. ☺

Mi amiga, Katarina, fue a Orlando para su trabajo. *(¿Adónde fue Katarina? ¿A Miami o a Orlando?)* Tuvo que reunirse con un grupo de colegas allí. *(¿Tuvo que reunirse con familia, con amigos o con personas de su trabajo?)* Pero también tuvo tiempo para divertirse un poco. *(¿Tuvo tiempo solamente para trabajar? ¿O tuvo tiempo para relajarse?)* Así que ella decidió visitar al Reino Mágico de Disney el viernes, un día antes de salir. *(¿Adónde decidió ir Katarina para divertirse? ¿Decidió ir al centro comercial o a un parque de diversiones?) (¿En qué día visitó el parque?)* Ella no condujo allí. Ella pudo tomar el tranvía que llevaba a la gente del hotel al parque. *(¿Fue Katarina al parque en su carro? ¿Cómo llegó Katarina al parque?)* Anduvo mucho ese día porque buscaba su montaña rusa favorita – el "Matterhorn". *(¿Por qué anduvo mucho Katarina? ¿Buscaba un restaurante o una atracción específica?)*. Ella pudo andar en muchas atracciones, pero no vio al "Matterhorn". *(¿Anduvo Katarina en otras atracciones o solamente anduvo en el "Matterhorn"?)* Por fin, ella pidió ayuda del empleado muy simpático del parque. Él se llamaba Cristóbal, y de él, Katarina supo la respuesta de por qué no pudo encontrar al "Matterhorn." *(¿De quién pidió ayuda Katarina? ¿De un empleado del Reino Mágico o con su amigo?)*. El empleado le dijo a Katrina que el "Matterhorn" no estaba en el Reino Mágico. Él le dijo que el "Matterhorn" sólo estaba en Disneylandia. *(¿Qué supo Katarina? ¿Supo que el "Matterhorn" estaba en otra parte del parque o que la atracción no estaba en el parque?)* Katarina estuvo un poco triste después de oír que su atracción favorita no estaba en el parque. *(¿Estuvo enojada o triste Katarina? ¿Por qué estuvo triste?)* Pero todavía se divirtió en las otras atracciones. Aunque había mucha genta en líneas largas, Katarina anduvo en muchas montañas rusas y vio unos espectáculos cómicos y bonitos. *(¿Eran largas o cortas las líneas para las atracciones? ¿Se divirtió o no se divirtió Katarina?)* A las diez, miró los fuegos artificiales, y escuchó la música. Después, a las diez y media, ella salió. *(¿Tuvo o no tuvo tiempo Katarina para mirar el espectáculo de fuegos artificiales?)* Ella no quiso gastar mucho dinero, así que no entró en las tiendas y no trajo ningún recuerdo. Sólo trajo el recuerdo de un día feliz en el Reino Mágico. *(¿Compró o no compró Katarina unos recuerdos? ¿Por qué no compró recuerdos de las tiendas?)*

Práctica 3.11

Look back over all the verbs in the preterite tense (pages 18-24). Write sentences that express five things you did yesterday. Try to add as much detail as possible. For example, you might include at what time you did the activity. Or you might include some descriptive words.

Ejemplo: (Yo) me vestí en los pantalones cortos y blancos con una camiseta gris a las siete y cuarto de la mañana.

1. _____

_____

2. _____

_____

3. _____

_____

4. _____

_____

5. _____

_____

Práctica 3.12

Now, look back again over the entire preterite tense (pages 18-24) and create five questions for your partner to answer. Choose five different activities, and ask if he/she did those activities yesterday.

Ejemplo: ¿Fuiste a un lugar interesante ayer?
Ejemplo: ¿Visitaste a un(a) amigo(a) ayer?

1. ¿_____

_____?

2. ¿_____

_____?

3. ¿_____

_____?

4. ¿_____

_____?

5. ¿_____

_____?

Preterite or Imperfect???

❖ Many people have difficulty determining when to use the preterite or imperfect tense. In English, we don't have anything like this to consider. We will try a few practice paragraphs to determine the difference between the two. But, often, either one may be gramatically correct. It is often a speaker or writer's choice, depending on the meaning he/she wishes to convey.

❖ Remember, the preterite is used when the speaker knows when the action began and ended. The imperfect is used if the speaker doesn't know or care when the action began or ended.

Práctica 3.13

Read the following paragraph in English. Then, read the paragraph again in Spanish, adding in the missing verbs. Decide if the verb should be in the preterite (you know when the action began and ended) or in the imperfect (you don't know ... or care... when the action began or ended).

> When I **was** young, I **lived** in a small house in the suburbs. My dad **used to take** me to school every morning. My school **was** close to my house, but I **didn't like** to walk alone. But one day, I **decided** to walk with my neighbor to the school. Her name **was** Rosita and she **lived** in the house across the street from mine.
>
> On that day, it **was** very cold in the morning. I **put on** my jacket and black boots before leaving the house. I **went** to Rosita's house and **knocked** on the door. She immediately **opened** the door and **smiled**. Her mom **said goodbye** and she **closed** the door. Rosita and I **walked** for one block. Then, we **saw** our friend, Ana and her brother, José. Ana and her brother always **used to walk** to school together. We all **started** to walk together. Then, it **started** to rain. We **laughed** and **ran** as fast as possible towards the school.
>
> At that moment, my dad **arrived** in his car. We all **climbed** in his car and he **took** us to the school.

Cuando yo (fui, era) niña, yo (viví, vivía) en una casa pequeña en los suburbios. Mi papá me (llevó, llevaba) a la escuela cada mañana. Mi escuela (estuvo, estaba) cerca de mi casa pero a mí no me (gustó, gustaba) caminar sola. Pero un día, yo (decidí, decidía) caminar con mi vecina a la escuela. Ella (se llamó, se llamaba) Rosita y ella (vivió, vivía) en la casa enfrente de la mía.

Ese día, (hizo, hacía) mucho frío por la mañana. Yo(me puse, me ponía) la chaqueta y las botas negras antes de salir de la casa. Yo (fui, iba) a la casa de Rosita y (toqué, tocaba) a la puerta. Ella (abrió, abría) la puerta inmediatamente y (se sonrió, se sonreía). Su mamá (se despidió , se despedía) de nosotras y ella (cerró, cerraba) la puerta. Rosita y yo (caminamos, caminábamos) por una cuadra. Entonces, nosotras (vimos, veíamos) a nuestra amiga, Ana, y a su hermano, José. Ana y su hermano siempre (caminan, caminaban) juntos a la escuela. Todos nosotros (empezamos, empezábamos) a caminar juntos. Entonces, (empezó, empezaba) a llover. (Nos reímos, Nos reíamos) y (corrimos, corríamos) lo más rápido posible hacia la escuela.

En ese momento, mi papá (llegó, llegaba) en su carro. Nosotros nos (subimos, subíamos) en su carro y él nos (llevó, llevaba) a la escuela.

Práctica 3.14

Try another one! Read the following paragraph in English. Then, read the paragraph again in Spanish, adding in the missing verbs. Decide if the verb should be in the preterite (you know when the action began and ended) or in the imperfect (you don't know … or care… when the action began or ended).

When I **was** sixteen years old, I **went** to Peru to live with a Peruvian family. I **traveled** with an exchange program. Before leaving, I was very scared. I didn't **know** what to expect. I didn't **know** much about life in Peru or the culture of the people.

On the day I **left**, I **said goodbye** to my family and **traveled** in a plane to Miami. In Miami, we **learned** about some customs in Peru. For example, we **learned** that people kiss each other when they greet each other. We **learned** that the people eat the main meal of the day at 2:00 in the afternoon during the hours of their siesta when all stores are closed.

After two days in Miami, we **traveled** to Peru where I **met** my family. During the following months, I **attended** school, **met** many new friends, and **discovered** that the Peruvian people are very kind and friendly. One week, I **went** to Machu Pichu and **saw** the ruins of the ancient city on top of the Andes Mountains. It **was** beautiful and very interesting!

I **lived** in Peru for only three months, but I **learned** a lot. The trip **changed** my life forever.

Cuando yo (tuve, tenía) dieciséis años, yo (fui, iba) al Perú para vivir con una familia peruana. Yo (viajé, viajaba) con un programa de intercambio. Antes de salir, yo (tuve, tenía) mucho miedo. Yo no (supe, sabía) qué esperar. Yo no (supe, sabía) mucho de la vida en Perú ni de la cultura de la gente.

El día que yo (salí, salía) yo me (despedí, despedía) de mi familia y yo (viajé, viajaba) por avión hacia Miami. En Miami, nosotros (aprendimos, aprendíamos) de unas costumbres en Perú. Por ejemplo, nosotros (aprendimos, aprendíamos) que las personas se besan cuando se saludan. Nosotros (aprendimos, aprendíamos) que la gente come la comida principal cada día a las dos de la tarde durante las horas de su siesta cuando todas las tiendas están cerradas.

Después de dos días en Miami, nosotros (viajamos, viajábamos) al Perú donde yo (conocí, conocía) a mi familia. Durante los siguientes meses, yo (asistí, asistía) a la escuela, (conocí, conocía) a muchos nuevos amigos, y (descubrí, descubría) que los peruanos (fueron, eran) muy simpáticos y amables. Una semana, yo (fui, iba) a Machu Picchu y (vi, veía) las ruinas de la ciudad antigua encima de las montañas de los Andes. (Fue, Era) muy bonita e interesante.

Yo (viví, vivía) en Perú por solo tres meses, pero yo (aprendí, aprendía) mucho. El viaje (cambió, cambiaba) mi vida para siempre.

Práctica 3.15

Try this one! Change the infinitive to the preterite or imperfect based on the context of the sentence. ¡Buena suerte! This is a challenge!

Yesterday my friend Cynthia and I **went** to El Prado in Madrid. We **wanted** to see the painting, "Las meninas" by Diego Velázquez. It **was** a warm day and the line to enter the museum **was** long. **There were** many people waiting to see the beautiful works of art in this famous museum.	Ayer mi amiga Cintia y yo (1. ir) a El Prado en Madrid. Nosotros (2. querer) ver la pintura "Las meninas" por Diego Velázquez. (3. Ser) un día caliente y la cola para entrar en el museo (4. ser) larga. (5. Haber) mucha gente esperando para ver las bellas obras de arte en este museo famoso.
While we **were waiting** in line, a group of young people **arrived**. One woman **was wearing** a beautiful long red dress. She **was** a flamenco dancer! The young people in the group **were** street performers. Some passers-by **began** to form a circle around them, but we **managed** to see them from the line. The young men in the group **began** to play the guitar. The woman **tapped** her heels to the music and **spun** around. Two men, the "hand clappers" from the group **clapped** their hands. We all **listened** at **watched**.	Mientras nosotros (6. esperar) en la cola, un grupo de jóvenes (7. llegar). Una mujer (8. llevar) un vestido bonito, largo y rojo. ¡Ella (9. ser) bailadora de flamenco! Los jóvenes del grupo (10. ser) artistas callejeros. Unos transeúntes (11. empezar) a formar un círculo alrededor de ellos, pero nosotros (12. poder) verlos desde la cola. Los jóvenes del grupo (13. empezar) a tocar la guitarra. La mujer (14. taconear) a la música y (15. girar). Dos hombres, los "palmeros" del grupo, (16. hacer) palmas. Nosotros (17. escuchar) y (18. mirar).
The line **was** long, but we **enjoyed** ourselves thanks to the talents of those performers.	La cola (19. ser) larga, pero nosotros nos (20. divertir) gracias a los talentos de esos artistas callejeros.

1. _____

2. _____

3. _____

4. _____

5. _____

6. _____

7. _____

8. _____

9. _____

10. _____

11. _____

12. _____

13. _____

14. _____

15. _____

16. _____

17. _____

18. _____

19. _____

20. _____

Práctica 3.16

Look at the following picture and study what was going on during the bank robbery. Discuss the questions that follow with your partner. Use the bank of vocabulary below to help you in your responses.

The robbery = el robo	The thief = el ladrón	The gun = la pistola	The beanie/cap = la gorra
The telephone = el teléfono	To hide = esconder(se)	To raise one's hands = levantar las manos	The money = el dinero
The bills = los billetes	The counter = el mostrador	The coins = las monedas	The bank teller = la cajera/ el cajero
The disguise = el disfraz	Fake = artificial	Real = verdadero(a)	The mask = la máscara

1. ¿Cuántas personas trabajaban cuando el ladrón llegó al mostrador?
2. ¿Qué hicieron los tres cajeros cuando el ladrón sacó la pistola?
3. ¿Cómo sabes que los cajeros tenían miedo del hombre?
4. ¿Crees que la moneda y los billetas ya estaban en el mostrador antes de que llegó el ladrón? ¿O crees que pusieron todo el dinero en el mostrador porque el ladrón les ordenó hacerlo?
5. ¿Por qué llevaba el ladrón la máscara? ¿Por qué llevaba una gorra el ladrón?
6. ¿A quién llamó por teléfono la cajera? ¿Con quién habló? ¿Crees que hizo la llamada telefónica cuando el ladrón apareció o que ya hablaba cuando él entró en el banco?

Chapter 4
What's "It" to Ya?
Direct and Indirect Object Pronouns

Object pronouns are used often in conversations. A pronoun is simply a word that takes the place of a noun, and, though you can survive with not knowing how to use them, you may sound a bit like a stuffy robot if you don't. Read these exchanges aloud with your partner:

Diálogo 4.1

Maestra:	Diego, tienes tu pluma, papel y libro?
Diego:	Sí, Señora, tengo mi pluma, papel y libro en mi mochila.
Maestra:	¿Y dónde pusiste tu mochila?
Diego:	Puse mi mochila en la clase.

Diálogo 4.2

Maestra:	Diego, tienes tu pluma, papel y libro?
Diego:	Sí, Señora, los tengo en mi mochila.
Maestra:	¿Y dónde pusiste tu mochila?
Diego:	La puse en la clase.

In the first dialogue, Diego repeats the direct object nouns of the sentence and sounds a bit like the stuffy robot repeating after the teacher. But in the second dialogue, he uses the direct object pronouns "them" and "it" to respond.

Try these:

Diálogo 4.3

Miguel:	Ana, ¿le vas a dejar la propina al mesero?
Ana:	Sí, Miguel. Ya le dejé la propina al mesero.
Miguel:	Bueno, entonces, ¿quieres ir a ver la película ahora? Tengo el horario del cine aquí. ¿Quieres ver el horario del cine?
Ana:	Sí, quiero ver el horario del cine.

Diálogo 4.4

Miguel:	Ana, ¿le vas a dejar la propina al mesero?
Ana:	Sí, Miguel. Ya se la dejé.
Miguel:	Bueno, entonces, ¿quieres ir a ver la película ahora? Tengo el horario del cine aquí. ¿Lo quieres ver?
Ana:	Sí, quiero verlo.

In Dialogue 4.3, Ana repeats the direct and indirect object nouns. In Dialogue 4.4, she uses the pronouns to replace the nouns and sounds much less stuffy and robotic.

One of the most difficult parts of using object pronouns for non-natives is that we often have forgotten (or perhaps never learned) what object pronouns are or how we use them in English.

Stated most simply, the object nouns receive the action directly (Direct Objects) or indirectly (Indirect Objects).

It sounds easy and obvious, but it takes practice to recognize those object nouns/pronouns and the role they play in a sentence. So let's start by practicing finding object pronouns!

❖ **There are three steps to finding a Direct Object in a sentence:**
   1. Find the subject of the sentence
   2. Find the verb in the sentence
   3. Ask "who?" or "what?" after the subject and verb. The answer to the question is the direct object (because he/she/it etc. is "who" or "what" is receiving the action of the verb).

Práctica 4.1
Find the direct object in each sentence in English.

1. Suzy cooks Bob a cake.

    1. Subject = _____

    2. Verb = _____

    3. _____ _____ Who?/What? = _____
          subject   verb   Direct Object
    Careful! Suzy isn't a cannibal! ☺ What is it she is really cooking?

2. We are watching the old movies in the living room.

    1. Subject = _____

    2. Verb = _____ _____

    3. _____ _____ Who?/What? = _____
          subject   verb

    _____
    Direct Object

3. Juana saw Carlos and me yesterday in the store.

    1. Subject = _____

    2. Verb = _____

    3. _____ _____ Who?/What? =
             subject   verb

        _____
        Direct Object

4. I invited Tomás and Julia to the party.

    1. Subject = _____

    2. Verb = _____

    3. _____ _____ Who?/What? =
             subject   verb

        _____
        Direct Object

Práctica 4.2

Now, look at those sentences again, and let's change the Direct Object Noun to a pronoun in English.

1. Suzy cooks Bob *a cake*.

    Suzy cooks _____ for Bob.

    *Note that when we use the pronoun in English, the sentence order changes a bit.

2. We are watching *the old movies* in the living room.

    We are watching _____ in the living room.

3. Juana saw *Carlos and me* yesterday in the store.

    Juana saw _____ yesterday in the store.

4. I invited _Tomás and Julia_ to the party.

I invited _____ to the party.

❖ Now let's try the same exercises in Spanish!
❖ In order to change a direct object noun to a pronoun, we need to know the vocabulary words for those object pronouns! Just as we needed to know the words "it", "them", and "us" in English, we need to know the translations for those words in Spanish.

Here are the direct object pronouns in Spanish:

Singular	Plural
Me me	Us nos
You (informal) te	You guys (informal) os
You (formal) Him, Her, It lo la	You all (formal) Them los las

Práctica 4.3
Find the direct object noun in each Spanish sentence. Then, change the direct object noun to a direct object pronoun.

1. Katia tomó la aspirina.

1. Sujeto/Subject = _____

2. Verbo/Verb = _____

3. _____ _____ ¿Quién? / ¿Qué?
            Subject   Verb

(Who?/What?) = _____
                               Direct Object Noun
                                 = (D.O. Pronoun)   _____

2. Yo vi a Alicia y a Verónica en la escuela ayer.

    1. Sujeto/Subject = _____

    2. Verbo/Verb = _____

    3. _____ _____ ¿Quién? / ¿Qué?
             Subject   Verb

    (Who?/What?) = _____
                          Direct Object Noun
                               = (D.O. Pronoun)   _____

3. Mis amigos comprenden a mí muy bien.

    1. Sujeto/Subject = _____

    2. Verbo/Verb = _____

    3. _____ _____ ¿Quién? / ¿Qué?
             Subject   Verb

    (Who?/What?) = _____
                          Direct Object Noun
                               = (D.O. Pronoun)   _____

4. Uds. invitaron a mi hermano y a mí a cenar en el restaurante, ¿no?

    1. Sujeto/Subject = _____

    2. Verbo/Verb = _____

    3. _____ _____ ¿Quién? / ¿Qué?
             Subject   Verb

    (Who?/What?) = _____
                          Direct Object Noun
                               = (D.O. Pronoun)   _____

The sentence order is a little different in Spanish when we use object pronouns.

- ❖ In English, the object pronouns are placed after a verb (Marta invited <u>us</u> to the party).
- ❖ In Spanish, the object pronouns are generally placed BEFORE THE CONJUGATED VERB in a sentence. (Marta <u>nos</u> invitó a la fiesta)
- ❖ The object pronouns MAY be placed at the end of an infinitive … if there is one in the sentence. The pronoun is attached directly on to the end of the verb. (Marta va a invitar<u>nos</u> a la fiesta).

Práctica 4.4
Now, change the direct object nouns in the previous sentences to object pronouns.

1. Katia tomó la aspirina.

_____

English: _____

2. Yo vi a Alicia y a Verónica en la escuela ayer.

_____

English: _____

3. Mis amigos comprenden a mí muy bien.

_____

English: _____

4. Uds. invitaron a mi hermano y a mí a cenar en el restaurante, ¿no?

_____

_____

*English:*_____

_____

Práctica 4.5

Translate the following sentences. Use pronouns for the direct object in each sentence.

1. She sold it (the house= la casa) yesterday.

_____

2. We received them (the documents = los documentos) last night.

_____

3. Manuel, do you see her?

_____

4. I invited you to my party, Diego.

_____

5. Who wrote it. (the novel = la novela)?

_____

6. Do you understand me, Sir?

_____

7. I am going to read them. (the books = los libros)

_____

or

_____

8. I love you. (to love = amar or querer)

_____

9. Who told you, Susana?

_____

10. We are going to visit you all in the summer.

_____

or

_____

Práctica 4.6

Underline the direct object noun in each sentence. Then, take turns with your partner asking and answering the questions using a pronoun in place of the direct object noun.

1. ¿Viste a tus amigos hoy?

_____

2. ¿Bebiste (el) café esta mañana?

_____

3. ¿Explicó la maestra la lección?

_____

4. ¿Dónde pusiste tu libro de español?

_____

5. ¿Comprendes tú los pronombres directos?

_____

6. ¿Vas a estudiar el español esta noche?

_____

or

_____

- ❖ **There are four steps to finding an Indirect Object in a sentence:**
  1. Find the subject of the sentence
  2. Find the verb in the sentence
  3. Ask "who?" or "what?" after the subject and verb. The answer to the question is the direct object (because he/she/it etc. is "who" or "what" is receiving the action of the verb.
  4. Ask "to whom?" or "for whom?" after the subject, verb and direct object (if there is one). The answer to the question "to whom?" or "for whom?" will be the indirect object noun because the person indirectly received the action.

- ❖ Here's how it works:

   Ejemplo: My husband bought me flowers.
      1. Subject = My husband
      2. Verb = bought
      3. My husband bought who or what? = flowers
         (he didn't buy ME, of course! ☺)
         ("Flowers" are the direct object noun.)
      4. My husband bought flowers to whom or for whom? = for me
         ("for me" is the indirect object noun.)

Práctica 4.7
Find the direct object and indirect object in each sentence in English.

1. Suzy cooks Bob a cake.

   1. Subject = _____

   2. Verb = _____

   3. _____ _____ who?/what? = _____
           Subject   Verb   Direct Object

   4. _____ _____ _____
           Subject   Verb   Direct Object

      to whom?/ for whom? = _____ = Indirect Object Noun

2. We left the tip for the waiter.

    1. Subject = _____

    2. Verb = _____

    3. _____ _____ who?/what? = _____
           Subject   Verb   Direct Object

    4. _____ _____ _____
           Subject   Verb   Direct Object

        to whom?/ for whom? = _____ = Indirect Object Noun

3. I told you the truth.

    1. Subject = _____

    2. Verb = _____

    3. _____ _____ who?/what? = _____
           Subject   Verb   Direct Object

    4. _____ _____ _____
           Subject   Verb   Direct Object

        to whom?/ for whom? = _____ = Indirect Object Noun

4. She gave me the money.

    1. Subject = _____

    2. Verb = _____

    3. _____ _____ who?/what? = _____
           Subject   Verb   Direct Object

    4. _____ _____ _____
           Subject   Verb   Direct Object

        to whom?/ for whom? = _____ = Indirect Object Noun

5. I am going to write you a letter.

    1. Subject = _____

    2. Verb = _____

    3. _____ _____ who?/what? = _____
            Subject   Verb   Direct Object

    4. _____ _____ _____
            Subject   Verb   Direct Object

       to whom?/ for whom? = _____ = Indirect Object Noun

- ❖ Indirect object pronouns are used EVERY time there is an indirect object in the sentence. Whereas the direct object pronoun REPLACES a direct object noun, the indirect object pronoun does not replace an indirect object noun, but is used IN ADDITION TO the indirect object noun. The indirect object pronoun may stand alone without the indirect object noun, but the indirect object noun must always be accompanied by the corresponding pronoun.

- ❖ The indirect object pronouns are often considered "redundant pronouns" because they are used in addition to the indirect object noun.

Ejemplo:
1. Carolina le deja la propina al mesero. = *Carolina leaves the tip for the waiter.*
2. Carolina le deja la propina. = *Carolina leaves the tip for him.*
   - ❖ The indirect object pronoun in each sentence is "le" meaning "to him/for him"
   - ❖ These two sentences above may be written in either of these two ways, but should not be written without the "le" even when the information "al mesero" is present. "Al mesero" is included simply to clarify to whom or for whom the tip is being left.

Ejemplo:
1. A mí me gusta hablar en español.
2. Me gusta hablar en español.
   - ❖ Do these sentences look familiar to you? They should! You've already learned to use the indirect object pronouns when you learned to express likes and dislikes with the verb "gustar".

- ❖ "Me" is the indirect object pronoun meaning "to me". You used it with "gustar" to say that "speaking Spanish is pleasing to me".
- ❖ The "a mí" information was used just to emphasize to whom the activity was pleasing!
- ❖ You can include "a mí" ... that information is optional. But you can't leave out the indirect object pronoun "me".

Ejemplo:
1. Yo les dije la verdad a mis padres.
2. Yo les dije la verdad.
   - ❖ In the first sentence, "les" refers to "them". "A mis padres" is there to clarify to whom I told the truth.
   - ❖ In the second sentence, there is no indication of to whom "les" refers. We would have already had to establish in our conversation that we were talking about my parents so the listener or reader knew that "les" referred to my parents and not to some other "them".

Here are the indirect object pronouns in Spanish:

Singular	Plural
To/for me me	To/for us nos
To/for you (informal) te	To/for you guys (informal) os
To/for you (formal) To/for him, her, it le *If used before "lo", "la" ,"los" or "las"* se	To/for you all (formal) To them les *If used before "lo", "la" ,"los" or "las"* se

Práctica 4.8
Underline or circle the indirect object in each sentence. In the blank space provided, write the indirect object pronoun needed. After, translate the sentence to English to check for understanding.

Ejemplo: Mi mamá **nos** dio dinero <u>a mi hermano y a mí</u>.
                 My mom gave money to my brother and me.

1. Carlos _____ pide ayuda a sus amigos.

_____

2. Jorge y yo no _____ queremos decir el secreto a ti.

_____

3. Mi familia _____ mandó una invitación a vosotros.

_____

4. A mi amiga, Laura, _____ gustan los animales.

_____

5. Ella siempre _____ explica la lección al estudiante.

_____

Práctica 4.9
Underline or circle the indirect object in each of the questions. Then, take turns asking and answering the questions with your partner. Remember that if you've already established in the question to whom or for whom the action is done, you only need the indirect object pronoun.
(*Note: For now, do not change the direct object noun to a pronoun. We have to learn a little more before you can change both object nouns to pronouns!)

Ejemplo: ¿<u>Le</u> vas a decir el secreto <u>a Marlena</u>? (no)
                 No, no le voy a decir el secreto. (or) No, no voy a decirle el secreto.

Ejemplo: ¿<u>Me</u> escribes tú el poema <u>a mí</u>? (Sí)
                 Sí, (yo) te escribo el poema.

1. ¿Le diste tú el regalo a tu hermano para su cumpleaños? (sí)

_____

2. ¿Les explicó la maestra la lección a los estudiantes? (sí)

_____

3. ¿Vas tú a mandarme la invitación a mí? (no)

_____

4. ¿Nos escribiste tú la carta a mi mamá y a mí? (no)

_____

5. ¿Les di yo los documentos a Uds.? (sí)

_____

6. ¿Te entrego la tarea a ti? (sí)

_____

❖ To use both an indirect and direct object pronoun in a sentence, you simply place the indirect object pronoun BEFORE the direct object pronoun. (*To help you remember, just think of remembering your ID card... Indirect before Direct = I.D.)

❖ The pronouns may be placed before the conjugated verb (with the indirect pronoun before the direct) OR they may be attached onto the end of an infinitive if there is an infinitive verb in the sentence.

❖ When two pronouns are attached onto the end of the infinitive, an accent mark may be needed.
   • If two pronouns are attached onto the end of an infinitive, an accent mark is placed over the infinitive's ending vowel.
   • If one pronoun is added to an infinitive, no accent mark is required.

   Ejemplo:
   1. Alicia va a darte el dinero. (one pronoun added; no accent mark needed)
   2. Alicia va a dártelo. (two pronouns added; accent mark over vowel)
   3. Alicia va a decirte el secreto. (one pronoun added, no accent needed)
   4. Alicia va a decírtelo. (two pronouns added; accent placed over vowel)

❖ When "le" or "les" is used with the direct object pronouns "lo, la, los, or las", the "le" or "les" will change to "se". This is done so the speaker doesn't have a tongue-twister while repeating the consonant "l".

Ejemplo:

      1. ¿Le das el dinero al mesero?

         Sí, se lo doy. (Instead of "Sí, le lo doy")

Práctica 4.10

Circle the direct object noun, and underline the indirect object noun and pronoun in each of the sentences. Then, rewrite the sentences using object pronouns, and translate your new sentence to English.

Ejemplo:

    1. Mis padres me piden (ayuda.) a mí.➜ Mis padres me la piden.

    My parents ask me for it.

1. La estudiante le entrega la tarea a la maestra.

_____

2. Yo te doy el regalo a ti.

_____

3. Mis padres me compran el carro nuevo a mí.

_____

4. Uds. nos leen la historia a nosotros.

_____

5. Nosotros os mandamos la invitación a vosotros.

_____

6. La maestra les explica la lección a los estudiantes.

_____

Práctica 4.11

Circle the direct object noun and underline the indirect object noun and pronoun in each of the questions. Then, take turns asking and answering the questions with your partner using object pronouns in your response. Say how often you or someone else does or does not do the activity mentioned.

siempre = *always*	cada año/mes/ día/ minuto /segundo = *every year / month / day / minute / second*
rara vez = *rarely*	de vez en cuando = *once in a while*
nunca = *never*	jamás = *never, ever!*

Ejemplo: ¿Les das tú las flores a tus amigos? ➜ Rara vez se las doy.

1. ¿Le das besos a tu esposo/a?

_____

2. ¿Te compra tu esposo/a los regalos a ti?

_____

3. ¿Le preparas tú la cena a tu familia?

_____

4. ¿Te escribe tu esposo/a los poemas a ti?

_____

5. ¿Les dices tú los secretos a tus amigos?

_____

6. ¿Les das tú tu ropa vieja a las organizaciones caricativas (charities)?

_____

7. ¿Les cuentas tú los chistes a tus amigos?

_____

8. ¿Te dan tus padres consejos (advice)?

_____

9. ¿Les das tú los consejos a tus hijos o a tus amigos?

_____

10. ¿Les traes tú comida a tus amigos cuando vas a una fiesta en su casa?

_____

_____

Práctica 4.12
With your partner, practice using indirect and direct object pronouns by asking your partner for items he/she might have in his/her backpack, purse or bag. Then trade off items by asking your partner to hand it/them to you. Read the following dialogues and then follow the pattern with your partner.

Ejemplo #1:
Estudiante A: ¿Tienes una pluma en tu mochila?
Estudiante B: Sí, la tengo. Te la doy. (gives pen to partner)
Estudiante A: Gracias por dármela.

Ejemplo #2
Estudiante B: ¿Tienes un diccionario en tu mochila?
Estudiante A: No, no lo tengo. No puedo dártelo.
Estudiante B: ¿Trajiste una hoja de papel?
Estudiante A: Sí la traje. Te la doy. (gives paper to partner)

Afterwards, if you want to keep practicing, you can request the items back. Follow this example:

Ejemplo #3
Estudiante A: ¿Me puedes dar mi pluma?
Estudiante B: Sí, te la doy.
Estudiante A: Gracias por devolvérmela.

Use the following list of vocabulary for ideas of things to ask for from your partner:

The sheet of paper = la hoja de papel	The pen = la pluma	The pencil = el lápiz	The eraser = el borrador	The notebook = el cuaderno	The tape = la cinta
The paperclip = el clip	The lipstick = el lápiz labial	The bandaid = la curita	The bottle of water = la botella de agua	The battery = la batería	The scisssors = las tijeras
The cell phone = el teléfono celular	The tissue = el tisú	The hair brush = el cepillo	The comb = el peine	The nail file = la lima de uñas	The nail polish = el esmalte de uñas
The coins = las monedas	The dollar bill = el dólar	The mirror = el espejo	The check book = el talonario de cheques	The calculator = la calculadora	The camera = la cámara
The glue = el pegamento	The pad of paper = la tableta de papel	The magazine = la revista	The rubber band = la liga	The photo = la foto	The hand lotion = la loción

Estudiante A: ¿Tienes _____?

Estudiante B: Sí, _____ tengo. _____ _____ doy. (give item to partner)

Estudiante A: Gracias por _____.

Estudiante B: ¿Tienes _____?

Estudiante A: No, no _____ tengo. No puedo _____.

Estudiante B: ¿Trajiste _____?

Estudiante A: Sí _____ traje. _____ _____ doy. (give item to partner)

Estudiante A: ¿Me puedes dar mi(s) _____?

Estudiante B: Sí, _____ _____ doy.

Estudiante A: Gracias por _____.

Práctica 4.13

Look at the following picture and the questions that follow on the next page. With your partner, discuss the answers you would give about what is happening. Use the vocabulary to help you. **Remember "Acabar de + infinitive" means "someone just finished doing something". (Acabo de cenar = I just finished eating)**

The engagement ring = el anillo de compromiso	The man = el hombre	The woman = la mujer	The flowers = las flores	The table = la mesa	The centerpiece = el centro de mesa
To kneel = arrodillar(se)	To propose = proponer	The dress = el vestido	The wedding = la boda	To say = decir	The diamond = el diamante
To marry = casar(se)	Will you marry me = ¿Quieres casarte conmigo?	The tablecloth = el mantel	The bottle = la botella	The money = el dinero	The life savings = los ahorros de la vida
The candlesticks= los candeleros	The ice bucket = La hielera	The flame = la llama	The champagne = la champaña	To smile = sonreír (e-i)	The candles = las velas

1. ¿Dónde están las dos personas?

2. ¿Qué hay en la mesa?

3. ¿Qué le da el hombre a la mujer?

4. ¿Por qué se arrodilla el hombre?

5. ¿Es un restaurante elegante o simple? ¿Cómo sabes?

6. ¿Hay flores en la mesa?

7. ¿Crees que la mujer le va a decir "sí" o "no"? ¿Por qué?

8. ¿Crees que los dos van a comer o ya acaban de comer?

9. ¿Qué van a tomar para celebrar?

10. ¿Cuánto le va a costar al hombre esta noche?

Práctica 4.14

Study the words in the list below. Then, look at the following picture and the questions that follow on the next page. With your partner, discuss your ideas about what is happening. Use the vocabulary to help you. **Remember "Acabar de + infinitive" means "someone just finished doing something". (Acabo de cenar = I just finished eating)**

The birthday party = la fiesta de cumpleaños	The family = la familia	The balloons = los globos	The cake = el pastel / la torta
The candles = las velas	To celebrate = celebrar	The plates = los platos	The cups = las tazas
The gift = el regalo	The waiter = el mesero	The tablecloth = el mantel	The flames= las llamas
To be (#) years old = tener (#) años	The birthday boy/girl = el/la cumpleañero/a	Dejected = desanimado(a)	Excited = Emocionado(a)
The table = la mesa	The silverware= los cubiertos	The main course = el plato principal	To bring = traer
The apron = el delantal	To make a wish = pedir un deseo	To complete, fulfill (to turn ____ years old) = cumplir	Lit = ecendido(a)

1. ¿Qué celebra la familia? ¿Cómo sabes?

2. ¿Van a comer el plato principal o acaban de comerlo las personas?

3. ¿Dónde están? ¿En una casa o en un restaurante? ¿Cómo sabes?

4. ¿Qué les trae el hombre a las personas sentadas en la mesa?

5. ¿Quién es el hombre con el pastel? ¿Es el tío o el mesero?

6. ¿Están desanimadas o emocionadas las personas en la mesa?

7. ¿Le trajeron los padres regalos a la niña?

8. ¿Están encendidas las velas en el pastel?

9. ¿Crees que la cumpleañera va a pedir un deseo?

10. ¿Cuántos años va a cumplir la cumpleañera?

Chapter 5
Mirror, Mirror on the Wall...
Here's the Fairest Pronoun of Them All
Reflexive Pronouns

Reflexive pronouns are used much like the direct and indirect object pronouns. The reflexive pronoun is used whenever the subject and receiver of the action are the same person. It is much like a reflection in a mirror – the person doing the action also receives the action ... reflected right back at him/her.

You might think of the reflexive pronoun, in part, this way: If you find the direct or indirect object is the same person as the subject of the sentence, the verb requires a reflexive pronoun.

Read these examples and note the roles of the direct, indirect, and reflexive pronouns.

Direct Object Pronoun: Yo lo leo. *(I read it)*
Indirect Object Pronoun: Yo le leo el libro. *(I read the book to him/her)*
Reflexive Pronoun: Yo me leo el libro. *(I read the book to myself)*

❖ Often times, the reflexive pronoun can be translated to English as "to oneself". *Read these examples:*

Direct Object Pronoun: Él la ve. *(He sees her.)*
Reflexive Pronoun: Él se ve. *(He sees himself.)*

Direct Object Pronoun: Ella lo escucha. *(She listens to to him/to you, formal.)*
Reflexive Pronoun: Ella se habla. *(She talks to herself.)*

Indirect Object Pronoun: La mamá le da el juguete al niño. *(The mom gives the little boy a toy.)*
Reflexive Pronoun: El niño se viste. *(The little boy dresses himself.)*

Indirect Object Pronoun: La abuela le acuesta a la niña para la mamá . *(The grandma puts the little girl to bed for her mom.)*
Reflexive Pronoun: La mamá se acuesta. *(The mom goes to bed / puts herself to bed.)*

Indirect Object Pronoun: Tu esposo te despierta. *(Your husband wakes you up.)*
Reflexive Pronoun: Tú te despiertas. *(You wake up... on your own or to an alarm.)*

❖ Reflexive pronouns may also imply the meaning "to get" or "to become" to the translation.

Read these examples:
- Ella **se casa** con el hombre de sus sueños. *(She is getting married to the man of her dreams.)*
- Los niños **se perdieron** en el bosque. *(The kids got lost in the forest.)*
- Los pasajeros **se enfermaron**. *(The passengers became sick.)*
- **Me levanto** a las seis de la mañana. *(I get up at 6:00 am.)*
- El niño **se desviste** antes de acostarse. *(The little boy gets undressed before going to bed.)*

Here are the reflexive pronouns

To me, to myself	To us, to ourselves
me	nos
To you, to yourself (informal)	To you guys, to yourselves (informal)
te	os
To him, to himself To her, to herself To you, to yourself (formal) se	To them, to themselves To yourselves (formal) se

❖ Almost any activity/verb can be made reflexive – if it's an action one would do upon or to oneself.

❖ Just like the other object pronouns, the reflexive pronoun is placed either before the conjugated verb or attached onto the end of an infinitive if there is one in the sentence.

❖ If there are multiple pronouns in one sentence, the reflexive always comes first. (RID = Reflexive, Indirect, Direct)

Práctica 5.1

Translate the following sentences to Spanish.

1. I am writing myself a letter.

_____

2. She saw herself in the mirror (el espejo).

_____

3. We talk to each other (to ourselves) in Spanish.

_____

4. Do you love yourself?

_____

5. He hears himself.

_____

Here is a list of high-frequency verbs that are often used in the reflexive that we haven't learned before

Acercarse (a)	To approach
Acostarse	To go to bed
Bañarse	To bathe; to take a bath
Callarse	To quiet oneself; to hush up
Calmarse	To calm down
Cepillarse	To brush (hair or teeth)
Cortarse	To cut; to get cut
Cuidarse de	To take care of oneself
Despertarse	To wake up
Desvestirse	To get undressed
Divertirse	To have fun; to enjoy oneself
Esconderse	To hide (oneself)
Lavarse	To wash (a part of one's body)
Levantarse	To get up; to stand up
Llamarse	To call oneself (to state someone's name)

Maquillarse	To put on makeup
Pararse	To stop oneself; to stop
Peinarse	To comb
Perderse	To get lost
Ponerse	To put on; to become (sick)
Probarse	To try on
Quitarse	To take off (an item of clothing)
Relajarse	To relax
Reunirse	To gather; to get together
Sentarse	To sit down
Vestirse	To get dressed

Práctica 5.2

Look at the picture below. Then discuss your answers to the questions from the next page with your partner.

61

1. ¿Es de la mañana o de la noche en el dibujo? ¿Cómo sabes?
2. En el dormitorio, ¿se viste el niño o lo viste su papá al niño?
3. ¿Qué hacen las personas en el baño? ¿Crees que el niño se afeitó o no?
4. ¿Qué hace la mujer en la sala?
5. ¿Quién les sirve el desayuno a los niños?
6. ¿Crees que el niño sentado a la derecha de la mesa le va a dar su comida al gato?

Práctica 5.3
Look at the picture below. Then discuss your answers to the questions that follow with your partner.

1. ¿Es de la mañana o de la noche en el dibujo? ¿Cómo sabes?
2. ¿Qué hace la persona en el baño?
3. ¿Por qué se arrodilla el niño en el dormitorio? ¿Le va a proponer o le reza a Dios?
4. ¿Por qué está la mamá en el dormitorio?
5. ¿Qué hace el hombre en el sillón en la sala? ¿Mira el programa en la televisión?
6. ¿Apaga o enciende la luz el hombre en la cocina? ¿Qué va a hacer el hombre?

Here is a list of some high-frequency verbs that often require the use of the reflexive pronoun but do not translate to English with the idea of "to oneself"

Aburrirse	To get bored
Acordarse (de)	To remember
Alojarse	To stay; to be lodged; to be housed
Apresurarse (a)	To hurry to
Aprovecharse (de)	To take advantage (of)
Asustarse (de)	To be scared of
Atreverse (a)	To dare (to)
Burlarse (de)	To make fun (of)
Caerse	To fall down
Cansarse	To get tired
Casarse (con)	To get married (to)
Darse cuenta (de)	To realize
Desayunarse	To eat breakfast
Desmayarse	To faint
Despedirse (de)	To say goodbye (to)
Dormirse	To fall asleep
Encontrarse (con)	To encounter; to meet up (with)
Enojarse (con)	To get mad (at)
Equivocarse	To make an error or mistake
Fijarse (en)	To stare (at); to notice
Irse	To go away, leave
Morirse	To die
Olvidarse (de)	To forget (about)
Parecerse (a)	To look like, resemble
Pelearse	To fight
Quedarse	To stay, remain
Quejarse (de)	To complain (about)
Reírse (de)	To laugh (at)
Rendirse	To give up
Sentirse	To regret; to feel
Sonreírse	To smile
Tratarse (de)	To be about; to concern; to be a question of

Práctica 5.4

Decide with your partner who will be "Lector(a) A" and who will be "Lector(a) B". If you are "Lector(a) A", you will read the story from Práctica 5.4 and ask your partner the corresponding questions. If you are "Lector(a) B" you will read the story from Práctica 5.5 and ask your partner the corresponding questions.

Before reading, follow these steps:
1. Read the English translation silently to yourself first.
2. Think of gestures you can use to convey the meaning as you read the story in Spanish to your partner. What gestures or actions could you make while reading to help him/her understand what is happening? Alternatively, you could sketch the actions of each part of the story. Focus on specific vocabulary words or phrases that your partner may struggle with understanding.
3. Read the Spanish version of your story aloud to your partner. Don't race through the words, and make sure you include either gestures or sketches/pictures to help your partner understand the words and ideas as you are reading.

For Reader A:

I have a friend whose name is Oliviana. Oliviana is very hard working and diligent. She is also very punctual. Oliviana always goes to bed early and wakes up early. She never ever arrives late to an event. So, we laugh at her for what happened when she took a trip to the Dominican Republic last year.

Last year Oliviana went away to the Dominican Republic for her job. She stayed in a very elegant hotel in Punta Cana. She told me that the bed in the hotel was the most comfortable bed in the entire world. The first night, she went to bed early, as usual, but she didn't fall asleep until two o'clock in the morning. She couldn't fall asleep because the family that was staying in the room next to her room was talking in loud voices all night. The kids were fighting and the parents were shouting at them. But at 2:00am, they calmed down and everything was tranquil.

But poor Oliviana woke up very late in the morning for having fallen asleep so late and also because she forgot to set the alarm clock. It was 9:30 when she woke up, and the meeting with her colleagues began at 8:00am. She hurried to the office. When she arrived, she noticed that no one was there. She decided to return to the hotel to call her colleagues.

Upon arriving at the hotel, she passed by the swimming pool. There she met up with all her colleagues. They were swimming happily in the pool, and they invited her to swim with them and to enjoy the beautiful day with them. At that moment, Oliviana realized that sometimes it is better to arrive late.

Para "Lector(a) A":

Tengo una amiga que se llama Oliviana. Oliviana es muy trabajadora y diligente. También es muy puntual. Oliviana siempre se acuesta y se levanta temprano. Ella jamás llega tarde a un evento. Por eso, nos burlamos de ella por lo que ocurrió cuando ella hizo un viaje a la República Dominicana el año pasado.

El año pasado, Oliviana se fue a la República Dominicana para su trabajo. Ella se alojó en un hotel muy elegante en Punta Cana. Ella me dijo que la cama del hotel era la cama más confortable de todas del mundo. La primera noche, ella se acostó temprano, como de costumbre, pero no se durmió hasta las dos de la mañana. No pudo dormirse porque la familia que se alojaba en el cuarto al lado del cuarto de ella hablaba en voces altas toda la noche. Los niños se peleaban y los padres les gritaban. Pero a las dos de la mañana, se calmaron y todo era tranquilo.

Pero, pobre Oliviana, se despertó muy tarde por la mañana por dormirse tan tarde y también porque se olvidó de poner el despertador. Eran las nueve y media cuando se despertó, y la reunión con sus colegas empezó a las ocho. Ella se apresuró a la oficina. Cuando llegó, se fijo que nadie estaba allí. Decidió volver a su hotel para llamar a sus colegas.

Al llegar al hotel, pasó por la piscina. Allí, se encontró con todos sus colegas. Ellos estaban nadando felizmente en la piscina, y la invitaron a nadar con ellos y disfrutar el día bonito con ellos. En ese momento, Oliviana se dio cuenta de que a veces es mejor llegar tarde.

Preguntas:

1. ¿Cómo se llama la personaje principal del cuento? ¿Se llama Yolanda u Oliviana?

2. ¿Cómo es ella? ¿Es trabajadora o perezosa?

3. ¿Dónde se alojó Oliviana?

4. ¿Se acostó tarde Oliviana la primera noche en el hotel?

5. ¿Por qué no se durmió Oliviana hasta muy tarde?

6. Oliviana no puso el despertador, pero ¿qué otra razón hay por no despertarse a tiempo en la mañana?

7. ¿A qué hora se despertó Oliviana?

8. ¿A qué hora empezó la reunión de la oficina?

9. ¿Dónde estaban todos sus colegas cuando Oliviana se encontró con ellos?

10. ¿Por qué se dio cuenta Oliviana de que a veces es mejor llegar tarde?

Práctica 5.4

If you are "Lector(a) B" you will read the story from this "práctica" and ask your partner the corresponding questions.

Before reading, follow these steps:

1. Read the English translation silently to yourself first.

2. Think of gestures you can use to convey the meaning as you read the story in Spanish to your partner. What gestures or actions could you make while reading to help him/her understand what is happening? Alternatively, you could sketch the actions of each part of the story. Focus on specific vocabulary words or phrases that your partner may struggle with understanding.

3. Read the Spanish version of your story aloud to your partner. Don't race through the words, and make sure you include either gestures or sketches/pictures to help your partner understand the words and ideas as you are reading.

For Reader B:

My friend, George, traveled to Aguascalientes, Mexico in November. He arrived on the 1st of November and he stayed in a simple and clean hotel near Madero Avenue. He arrived late at night and went directly to his hotel. He went to bed right away because he wanted to get up early the next day in order to see the most possible. But he couldn't fall asleep because he heard a lot of noise in the streets. He got up, got dressed, and went down the stairs quickly in order to see what was going on outside.

He went out to the street. He got scared and almost fainted when he stared at the incredible scene in the street. He saw a ton of pretty colors, and amongst the colors there were many people. But they weren't people – they were skeletons and the skeletons were dancing in the streets. George thought about the date – it was the 1st of November.

66

It wasn't the thirty first of October but he believed they were celebrating Halloween. But he stared at the skeletons. They weren't scary; they were funny. They were smiling and laughing, and were wearing colorful clothing.

At that moment, George saw a photo of a skull. The skull was of a woman who was wearing an elegant hat with a flower. Upon seeing this skull, George realized that he made a mistake. They weren't celebrating Halloween. They were celebrating Day of the Dead. George remembered this skull that was called "La Catrina". It was a famous painting by José Guadalupe Posada and many people used this painting and skull to represent the ideas of Day of the Dead. In the painting the skull was wearing an elegant hat because La Catrina represented and made fun of the rich.

George abandoned his plans of sleeping and followed the people to the cemetery. There he saw the altars that the families were decorating. George told me it was an unforgettable experience.

Para "Lector(a) B":

Mi amigo, Jorge, viajó a Aguascalientes, México en noviembre. Llegó el primero de noviembre y se alojó en un hotel simple y limpio cerca de la Avenida Madero. Llegó tarde por la noche y fue directamente a su hotel. Se acostó en seguida porque quería levantarse temprano el próximo día para ver todo lo más posible. Pero no pudo dormirse porque oyó mucho ruido en las calles. Se levantó, se vistió, y bajó las escaleras rápidamente para ver lo que pasaba afuera.

Salió a la calle. Se asustó y casi se desmayó cuando se fijó en la escena increíble en la calle. Vio un montón de colores bonitos, y entre los colores había muchas personas. Pero no eran personas – eran esqueletos y los esqueletos bailaban en las calles. Jorge pensó en la fecha – era el primero de noviembre. No era el treinta y uno de octubre pero creía que celebraban la noche de brujas (o Halloween). Pero se fijó en los esqueletos. No eran espantosos, eran cómicos. Se sonreían y llevaban ropa llena de colores.

En ese momento Jorge vio una foto de una calavera. La calavera era de una mujer que llevaba un sombrero muy elegante con una flor. Al ver esta calavera, Jorge se dio cuenta de que se equivocó. No celebraban la noche de brujas. Celebraban el día de los muertos. Jorge se acordó de esta calavera que se llamaba "La Catrina". Fue una pintura famosa de José Guadalupe Posada y muchas personas usaban esta pintura y calavera para representar las ideas del día de los muertos. En la pintura la calavera llevaba un sombrero elegante porque La Catrina representaba y se burlaba de los ricos.

Jorge abandonó sus planes de dormir y siguió a la gente al cementerio. Allí vio los altares que decoraban las familias. Jorge me dijo que era una experiencia inolvidable.

Preguntas:

1. ¿Adónde fue Jorge?
2. ¿En qué mes viajó? ¿Te acuerdas tú la fecha específica?

3. ¿Llegó Jorge por la mañana o por la noche?

4. ¿Al llegar al hotel iba a acostarse o levantarse Jorge?

5. ¿Qué vio Jorge cuando llegó a la calle?

6. ¿Qué creía Jorge que estaban celebrando las personas?

7. ¿En realidad, qué celebraban?

8. Dicen que en el día de los muertos la gente usa esqueletos y máscaras para burlarse de la muerte. ¿Qué vio Jorge que corresponde a esta idea?

9. ¿Cómo es la pintura "La Catrina" y quién la pintó?

10. ¿Qué hacían las familias en el cementerio?

Chapter 6
Let's Get It Done!
Commands and Pronouns

We hear and give commands frequently in Spanish. We use commands to tell people what to do or what not to do. In order to make a request, we can't conjugate the verbs to the simple present tense. If we use the present tense, the action will be understood as a statement and not as a request.

Consider:
- Hablas en voz alta = *You speak/are speaking in a loud voice. (Meaning you are actually doing the action)*
  vs.
- Hable en voz alta = *Speak in a loud voice. (Meaning, the speaker is requesting that the other person speak in a loud voice. Whether or not the person does that action is unknown.)*

There are two types of commands
1. **Affirmative commands** in which the speaker/writer tells someone what TO DO
2. **Negative commands** in which the speaker/writer tells someone what NOT TO DO

We can give affirmative and negative commands to the following people:
- tú
- Ud.
- Uds.
- vosotros
- nosotros

We can only give commands in the present time. We can't tell someone to do something in the past (unless and until some magical time machine becomes available ☺) Therefore; we base the conjugation of the command form on the present tense. We just modify the present tense conjugation a little to let listener/reader know we are making a request.

*In this text, we will not explore the way to form the affirmative and negative command forms for "vosotros". Since it is only used in Spain, and because it is generally acceptable to give a command to a group of people with the formal form, we will focus on the use of "Uds." when giving a command to a group of people, even if they are all friends or younger children. If you travel to Spain and want to tell all your friends what to do or not to do, you may research more on the "vosotros" command form.

To form the AFFIRMATIVE "Tú" COMMAND (ONLY)

❖ Use the third person singular form (the él, ella, Ud. form) of the verb in the present tense.

Ejemplos:

1. Canta la canción. = *Sing the song.*
2. Toma el autobús. = *Take the bus.*
3. Corre a casa. = *Run home.*
4. Abre la ventana. = *Open the window.*

❖ The person would know that you are not saying that he, she, or you (formal) are doing the activity because, with a command, you are speaking directly to the person to whom you are making the request.

❖ **There are 8 irregular forms:**

Spanish Infinitive	Affirmative Command	English Translation
1. Decir	Di	Say, tell
2. Hacer	Haz	Do, make
3. Ir	Ve	Go
4. Poner	Pon	Put, place
5. Salir	Sal	Go out, leave
6. Ser	Sé	Be (*remember "DOCTOR")
7. Tener	Ten	Have (or "be" with expressions of "tener")
8. Venir	Ven	Come

Práctica 6.1

Your friend is telling you what you should do to live a healthy life. Translate the following commands he/she is giving you to English.

1. Come muchas verduras.

_____

2. Haz ejercicio.

_____

3. Participa en actividades que te hacen feliz.

_____

4. Pasa tiempo con amigos o familia.

_____

5. Sigue aprendiendo.

_____

Práctica 6.2

You are talking to your child about how to be successful at his/her new job. Change the infinitive to a command. Then, translate your advice to English.

Ejemplo: Ser diligente.
      Sé diligente
      Be diligent.

1. Llegar al trabajo a tiempo.

_____

_____

2. Tener cuidado con tu trabajo.

_____

_____

3. Escuchar las instrucciones.

_____

_____

4. Poner todos los documentos en un lugar seguro.

_____

_____

5. Hacer preguntas y decir la verdad.

_____

_____

6. Conocer a los secretarios y a tus colegas.

_____

_____

To form the NEGATIVE COMMAND FOR "Tú" and the AFFIRMATIVE AND NEGATIVE COMMANDS FOR "Ud.", "Uds.", and "Nosotros", follow these steps:

1. Find the "yo" form of the verb in the present tense
2. Drop the final ending "o" off of the conjugation and the following endings based on the person to whom you are speaking

	Tú (negative)	Ud.	Uds.	nosotros
-AR Verbs	- es	-e	-en	-emos
-ER and -IR Verbs	- as	-a	-an	-amos

Práctica 6.3

You are at a party. Give commands to the person/people indicated by changing the Spanish infinitive to a command.

1. the boss of one of your friends / *Tomar el vaso.* (Take the glass.)

_____

2. your colleagues from work / *Comer y disfrutar.* (Eat and enjoy.)

_____

3. your spouse / *No salir* (Don't leave.)

_____

4. the entire group including yourself / *Abrir los regalos.* (Let's open the gifts.)

_____

5. your boss / *No hacer el trabajo ahora.* / (Don't do the work now.)

_____

Irregular Command Conjugations

❖ Verbs that ended in –CAR, -GAR, and -ZAR will have a spelling change for all forms of the commands to maintain the sound of the infinitive ending. (Just like they did with the preterite tense)

Endings for verbs ending in –CAR, -GAR, -ZAR

Ending	Tú (negative)	Ud.	Uds.	nosotros
-CAR	-ques	-que	-quen	-quemos
-GAR	-gues	-gue	-guen	-guemos
-ZAR	-ces	-ce	-cen	-cemos

Práctica 6.4
Write the following commands according to the person indicated.

1. Don't arrive late. (tú)

_____

2. Have lunch with me. (Ud.)

_____

3. Look for my keys. (Uds.)

_____

4. Let's pay the bill. (nosotros)

_____

5. Don't cross the street. (Uds.)

_____

❖ Note that any "nosotros" command that ends with "-AR" or "-ER" will not have a stem change if it was a stem-changing verb in the present tense.

> _Ejemplos:_
> 1. contar – yo cuento
>   "let's count" = con**temos**
>
> 2. perder – yo pierdo
>   "let's not lose" = no per**damos**
>
> 3. almorzar – yo almuerzo
>   "let's have lunch" = almor**cemos**
>
> 4. mover = yo muevo
>   "let's move" = mo**vamos**

❖ Any "nosotros" command that ends with "-IR" _WILL_ have a stem change if it was a stem-changing verb in the present tense. "E" will change to "I" and "O" will change to "U".

> _Ejemplos:_
> 1. pedir – yo pido
>   "let's order" = p**i**damos
>
> 2. dormir – yo duermo
>   "let's sleep" = d**u**rmamos
>
> 3. mentir – yo miento
>   "let's not lie" = no m**i**ntamos
>
> 4. morir – yo muero
>   "let's not die" = no m**u**ramos

74

Práctica 6.5

You are suggesting to your friends what you should and shouldn't do today. Translate the following commands to Spanish.

1. Let's not order pizza. (pedir)

_____

2. Let's repeat the new vocabulary. (repetir)

_____

3. Let's not go to bed early. (acostarse)

_____

4. Let's have lunch in the restaurant. (almorzar)

_____

5. Let's begin early. (empezar)

_____

6. Let's not follow the rules. (seguir)

_____

7. Let's not compete. (competir)

_____

8. Let's laugh a lot. (reír)

_____

There are 5 completely irregular conjugations:

Spanish Infinitive	English	Tú (negative)	Ud.	Uds.	nosotros
1. Dar	Give/don't give	No des	Dé No dé	Den No den	Demos No demos
2. Estar	Be / don't be (PLACE)	No estés	Esté No esté	Estén No estén	Estemos No estemos
3. Ir	Go/don't go	No vayas	Vaya No vaya	Vayan No vayan	Vamos/ No vayamos
4. Saber	Know/don't know (usually used for "to memorize)	No sepas	Sepa No sepa	Sepan No sepan	Sepamos No sepamos
5. Ser	Be/ don't be (DOCTOR)	No seas	Sea No sea	Sean No sean	Seamos No seamos

Práctica 6.6

Write the following commands according to the person indicated. Decide if you would use the affirmative or negative command based on the information.

Ejemplo: Ir a la playa durante una tormenta. (Uds.)
   No vayan a la playa durante una tormenta.

1. Saber de memoria el vocabulario de este libro. (Uds.)

_____

2. Ir al trabajo durante las vacaciones. (Ud.)

_____

3. Darles las drogas a los niños. (tú)

_____

4. Ser antipáticos. (nosotros)

_____

5. Estar en la piscina mientras truena. (tú)

_____

6. Estar felices (Uds.)

_____

Práctica 6.7

Use the infinitive provided to create a command the doctor would give to the patient.
Ejemplo: jugar al voleibol ➔   No juegue Ud. al voleibol.

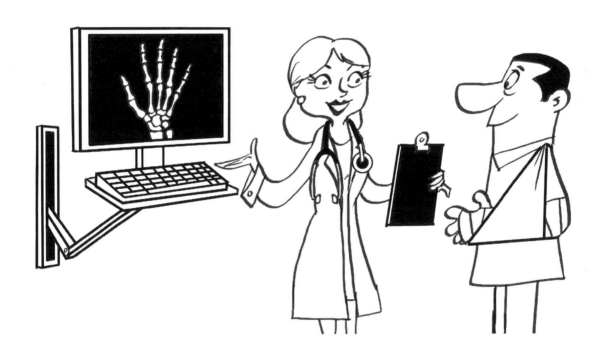

1. Escribir con la mano izquierda (left)=_____

2. Escribir con la mano derecha (right)= _____

3. Moverse la muñeca (wrist) = _____

4. Bañarse con la venda (bandage)= _____

5. Conducir un coche por una larga distancia = _____

   _____

6. Practicar el boxeo = _____

7. Tener cuidado = _____

8. Mantener limpia la venda = _____

9. Visitar la clínica en seis semanas = _____

_____

10. Andar en las montañas rusas = _____

When direct, indirect or reflexive pronouns are used with commands, the word order changes depending upon whether the command is affirmative or negative. The order of the pronouns, however, remains the same with indirect object pronouns before the direct (ID) or reflexive, indirect and then direct object pronouns (R.I.D.) if there is a reflexive pronoun.

❖ **With affirmative commands, the pronouns are attached onto the end of the command.**

Ejemplos:
1. Sell it (el carro) to him.
    Tú = Véndeselo.
    Ud. = Véndaselo.
    Uds. = Véndanselo.
    Nosotros = Vendámoselo

    • **Note:** We have to drop the final "s" of the nosotros conjugation before attaching pronouns "nos" or "se"

    • Vendamos + se + lo (dropped the "s" of the nosotros conjugation)

2. Write it (la carta) to us. (Uds.)

    Tú = Escríbenosla.
    Ud. = Escríbanosla.
    Uds. = Escríbannosla.
    Nosotros = Escribámonosla.

    • **Note:** We have to drop the final "s" of the nosotros conjugation before attaching pronouns "nos" or "se"

    • Escribamos + nos + la (dropped the "s" of the nosotros conjugation)

3. Give them the money.

> Tú = Dales el dinero.
> Ud. = Déles el dinero.
> Uds. = Denles el dinero.
> Nosotros = Démosles el dinero.
>
> • Note: We don't have to drop the final "s" of the nosotros conjugation because we didn't' attach pronouns "nos" or "se"

4. Go to bed!

> Tú = Acuéstate.
> Ud. = Acuéstese.
> Uds. = Acuéstense.
> Nosotros = Acostémonos (drop the "s" before the pronoun "nos")

❖ **When pronouns are added to the affirmative commands, an accent may be needed.**

- If one pronoun is added to a single syllable command, no accent mark is needed

    Ejemplos:
    1. Vete (tú) a la tienda. *(Go to the store.)*
    2. Ponlo (tú) en la mochila. *(Put it in the backpack.)*
    3. Denles (Uds.) el dinero. *(Give them the money.)*

- If two pronouns are added to a single syllable command, an accent mark is needed over the vowel that is stressed in the conjugation of the command itself.

    Ejemplos:
    1. Házmelo (tú). *(Make it for me.)* (*"Haz" is the stressed syllable of the command)*
    2. Dénmelo (Uds.). *(Give it to me.)* *("Den" is the stressed syllable of the command)*
    3. Dímelo (tú) *(Tell it to me.)* *("Di" is the stressed syllable of the command)*

- If one or two pronouns are added to a two or more syllable command, an accent mark must be placed over the vowel that is stressed in the conjugation of the command itself.

    Ejemplos:
    1. Váyase (Ud.) a la tienda. *(Go to the store.)* *("Va-ya" has the stress over "va" in the original command conjugation)*

2. Vístanse (Uds.) *(Get dressed.)* *("Vi-sta" has the stress over the "vi" in the original conjugation of the command)*
3. Vámonos (nosotros). *(Let's go.)* *("Va-mos" has the stress over the "va" in the original verb conjugation)*
4. Léemelo (tú). *(Read it to me.)* *("Le-e" has the stress over the "le" in the original conjugation of the command)*

❖ **With negative commands, the pronouns are placed before the conjugated form of the command.**

Ejemplos:
1. Don't sell it (el carro) to him.
    Tú = No se lo vendas.
    Ud. = No se lo venda.
    Uds. = No se lo vendan.
    Nosotros = No se lo vendamos.

2. Don't write it (la carta) to us. (Uds.)
    Tú = No nos la escribas.
    Ud. = No nos la escriba.
    Uds. = No nos la escriban.
    Nosotros = No nos la escribamos.

3. Don't give them the money.
    Tú = No les des el dinero.
    Ud. = No les dé el dinero.
    Uds. = No les den el dinero.
    Nosotros = No les demos el dinero.

Práctica 6.8
Translate the following commands to Spanish. Use pronouns for the words in parenthesis.
    Ejemplo: Let's sell it (the car) to them.
            Vendémoselo.

1. Juan, give it (el regalo) to us.

_____

2. Mr. Arroyo, please show it (la pintura) to me.

_____

3. Jorge y Manuel, don't tell it (el chiste) to us.

_____

4. Mr. and Mrs. Martínez, please sit down.

_____

5. Let's go to the beach!

_____

6. Carlitos, don't touch it (el vaso).

_____

7. Mom, don't do it (el trabajo) for me.

_____

8. Let's not fight.

_____

9. Verónica, read it (la historia) to me.

_____

10. Friends, don't buy them (los libros) for me.

_____

Práctica 6.9

You are a physical therapist working with a patient. The patient is asking you questions regarding what he should and should not do in order to keep his neck safe from further injury. Respond to his questions using commands and pronouns whenever possible.

Ejemplo: ¿Debo usar la cinta de correr?

Sí, úsela.

1. ¿Puedo levantar las pesas?

_____

2. ¿Puedo ir al gimnasio?

_____

3. ¿Debo acostarme y dormir en el suelo?

_____

4. ¿Puedo andar en las montañas rusas y rápidas (roller coasters)?

_____

5. ¿Puedo ponerme el hielo (ice)?

_____

6. ¿Puedo correr por las calles?

_____

7. ¿Puedo ir de compras?

_____

8. ¿Puedo llevar los tacones (heels) muy altos?

_____

Práctica 6.10

Look at the following pictures and corresponding names of the people in each picture.
Read the commands below and decide to whom each piece of advice should/would be given.

1. No corras en la calle.
2. Come muchas verduras.
3. No comas dulces.

4. Acuéstate temprano.
5. Póngase derecho. No se encorve.
6. Lleve los zapatos confortables.

Final note on the commands:

❖ Often when we give a command to "nosotros", we simply use the expression "vamos + a + infinitive" or simply "A + infinitive" to mean "let's ...(do an activity).
Here are three ways to say "Let's go swimming!"
   1. ¡Nademos!
   2. ¡Vamos a nadar!
   3. ¡A nadar!

Práctica 6.11

Imagine you're at a friend's house on the weekend, and you're suggesting ideas you two can do together. Write the three ways to give the following commands to "us".

1. Let's eat in a Mexican restaurant!

   a. _____

   b. _____

   c. _____

2. Let's watch a movie!

   a. _____

   b. _____

   c. _____

3. Let's walk to the park!

   a. _____

   b. _____

   c. _____

4. Let's practice Spanish!

   a. _____

   b. _____

   c. _____

Chapter 7
Are You in the Mood?
The Subjunctive

Whenever anyone expresses doubt, uncertainty, denial, desire or emotion about what might or might not happen, the subjunctive mood is required. The subjunctive is considered a mood, and not a tense, because the verb is reflecting the doubt or uncertainty of the speaker/writer.

So far we have learned to conjugate a verb in the indicative tenses. An indicative tense indicates when an action took place; it reports an event or information about an actual event that absolutely did or did not occur. We are stating facts about actions occurring or not occurring. But with the subjunctive, there is an unknown – there is uncertainty or as to whether or not the action will, or did, take place.

The reason the subjunctive is so difficult for non-natives is because we hardly use the subjunctive in English. The closest we have is with the "if" clauses - when we say things such as "If I were you…" or "If she were here with me…" The verb "were" is in the subjunctive because the speaker is demonstrating that "I am NOT you", and "she is NOT here with me".

Spanish uses the subjunctive far more often than we do in English. In Spanish, we use the subjunctive when a clause (or part of the sentence) involves any of these conditions:
- ❖ Desire
- ❖ Ignorance
- ❖ Impersonal opinion
- ❖ Unfinished action
- ❖ Vague or indefinite antecedent
- ❖ Maybe/perhaps
- ❖ "Even if"

Generally, but not always, there are two clauses in the sentence so that the structure looks something like this:

Subject #1 + Verb #1 + "que" + Subject #2 + Verb #2 (S1V1 + que + S2V2)

Verb #2 is usually the verb in the **SUBJUNCTIVE**

Verb #1 is usually the **TRIGGER** verb (a verb of DIES)

Remember, the subjunctive mood always involves some type of unknown or unlikely event. With the subjunctive, there is doubt, uncertainty, or an unlikeliness that the action ever took place or would ever take place.

Compare the following sentences where the first sentence is written in the indicative and the second sentence has a subjunctive verb highlighted.

Indicative Sentence	Subjunctive Sentence (subjunctive is highlighted)
1. Uds. vienen a mi fiesta. *You all are coming to my party.*	1. Yo espero que Uds. **vengan** a mi fiesta. *I hope that you **come** to my party.*
2. Nosotros estudiamos mucho. *We study often.*	2. Ella quiere que nosostros **estudiemos** mucho. *She wants us **to study** often.*
3. ¡Nosotros podemos hacerlo! *We can do it!*	3. Ellos dudan que nosotros **podamos** hacerlo. *They doubt that we **can** do it.*
4. Ellos están aquí. *They are here.*	4. Nosotros no creemos que ellos **estén** aquí. *We don't believe they **are** here.*
5. Me alojo en ese hotel. *I am staying in that hotel.*	5. Ella me avisó que **me alojara** en ese hotel. *She advised me **to stay** in that hotel.*
6. Tú estás contenta. *You are happy.*	6. Yo me alegro de que tú **estés** contenta. *I'm glad you **are** happy.*
7. Nosotros visitaríamos esa tienda. *We would visit that store.*	7. Si nosotros **estuviéramos** allí, nosotros visitaríamos esa tienda. *If we **were** there, we would visit that store.*
8. Tú no sabes la respuesta. *You don't know the answer.*	8. Yo no creo que tú **sepas** la respuesta. *I don't believe you **know** the answer.*
9. Nosotros estamos tristes. *We are sad.*	9. Nosotros estamos tristes que tú **salgas**. *We are sad that you **are leaving**.*
10. Tú comprendes el subjuntivo. *You understand the subjunctive.*	10. Es importante que tú **comprendas** el subjuntivo. *It's important that you **understand** the subjunctive.*
11. A Uds. les gusta la comida. *You all like the meal.*	11. ¡Ojalá que a Uds. les **guste** la comida! *Oh how I hope that you all **like** the meal!*

Note the following in each of the subjunctive sentences from the previous page:

- ❖ There is a change of subject.

- ❖ The verb that is not highlighted is often an action that is actually known (for example, in #1, I really am hoping; in #2 it is a fact that she is wanting... but whether or not you come to my party or we study is unknown. It's requested and hoped for, but not guaranteed to occur or not occur.

- ❖ The highlighted verb is the part that is contrary to fact or unknown (for example, in #7, we are NOT there so the situation is contrary to fact; in #10 it is unknown whether or not you will understand the subjunctive.

- ❖ If the highlighted verb is true and factual, we use the subjunctive for verb #2 because someone else is feeling an emotion about it (for example, in #6 you ARE happy, and I am glad about it. In #9 you are leaving, and we are sad about it.

Words that trigger wishes, emotions, impersonal observations, requests, doubts, denial, disbelief, and speculation are "trigger words" for the subjunctive. Let's shorten these ideas into four types of words... verbs of Doubt, Influence, Emotion, and Speculation (DIES)

Práctica 7.1
Decide if the following highlighted verbs would be written in the Indicative ("I") or the Subjunctive ("S"). Discuss why the verb would be Indicative or Subjunctive... is Doubt, Influence, Emotion or Speculation (DIES) involved? Check your answers in the back of the book for further information and clarification.

*Ejemplo: They want me **to listen** to the story.   = S (Influence)*

*Ejemplo: It's obvious that you all **are** very smart. = I (No doubt)*

1. My mom prefers that I **go to bed** early.   1. _____

2. She hopes that I **will arrive** on time.   2. _____

3. We know that she **is** a good student.   3. _____

4. They doubt that we **will study**.   4. _____

5. It is possible that she **isn't** here.   5. _____

6. We believe he **is** at the park right now.   6. _____

7. It is better that you all **come** tomorrow.   7. _____

8. We don't doubt that you **know** him.   8. _____

9. They are glad that we **are** here.   9. _____

10. She hopes **to live** in California.   10. _____

11. My teachers are afraid the tests **are** too hard.   11. _____

12. We want **to study** more.   12. _____

13. My friends tell me **to write** them letters.   13. _____

14. My friends tell me that I **am** nice.   14. _____

15. It's important that you all **give** me lots of chocolate.   15. _____

16. The administration forbids us **to write** on walls.   16. _____

17. I suggest that you **follow** directions.   17. _____

18. If I **were** you, I'd bring chocolate to the teacher.   18. _____

19. He prefers **to sit** there quietly.   19. _____

20. It is certain that it **will rain** tomorrow.   20. _____

21. I believe that he **is telling** the truth.   21. _____

22. I **hope** that the party is fun.   22. _____

23. The students hope that the finals **are** cancelled.   23. _____

24. We know that we need **to study** this information.   24. _____

25. The bathrooms in the restaurant **are** clean.   25. _____

26. She sees that he **is** angry.   26. _____

27. I beg you **to do** your work.   27. _____

28. My parents tell me **to listen**.   28. _____

29. They are not certain that we **are** nice people.   29. _____

30. I want to learn **to speak** Italian.   30. _____

31. I am sorry that you **don't like** this type of exercise.   31. _____

32. She will arrive as soon as the sun **sets**.   32. _____

33. I believe I will **pass** the test.   33. _____

34. I am looking for someone who **has** good speaking skills.   34. _____

35. Do you know anyone who **can** translate this sentence?   35. _____

36. Why do you doubt that I **can** learn this?   36. _____

So let's try this out in Spanish, shall we? First you'll need to recognize the vocabulary words that trigger wishes, emotions, impersonal observations, requests, doubts, denial, disbelief, and speculation... the verbs of Doubt, Influence, Emotion, and Speculation (DIES).

I. VERBS OF DOUBT

Dudar	To doubt
Es dudoso	It's doubtful
Es imposible	It's imposible
Es improbable	It's unlikely, improbable
Es incierto	It's uncertain
Es posible	It's possible
Es probable	It's probable
Negar (e-ie)	To deny
No creer	Not to believe
No estar seguro(a) de	Not to be sure
No pensar	Not to think
Puede ser	It may be
Quizás	Maybe
Tal vez	Perhaps

*Read each of the example sentences below for examples of verbs of **doubt** or uncertainty. While you read, cover the English translation in the right column. Have one partner read the first five sentences aloud to the other partner, and then trade so the other partner reads the last five sentences. See if your partner can give you the correct English translations to the Spanish sentences you read.*

Compañero(a) A:

1. No estoy seguro de que me comprendas bien.	1. I'm not sure you understand me well.
2. Es dudoso que el banco esté abierto hoy.	2. It's doubtful that the bank is open today.
3. ¿No crees que el autobús llegue a las tres?	3. Don't you think that the bus is arriving at 3:00?
4. Quizás mis amigos me llamen esta noche.	4. Maybe my friends will call me tonight.
5. No creemos que el guía sepa mucho de la historia.	5. We don't believe the guide knows much about history.

1. Es improbable que ella venga a la oficina hoy.	1. It's improbable that she is coming to the office today.
2. La mujer duda que el tren llegue a tiempo.	2. The woman doubts that the train arrives on time.
3. Puede ser que no haga calor mañana.	3. It might be that it's not going to be hot tomorrow.
4. Quizás no quieras acompañarme al cine.	4. Maybe you don't want to go with me to the movies.
5. Es incierto que él hable inglés.	5. It's uncertain that he speaks English.

II. VERBS OF INFLUENCE

Aconsejar	To advise
Decir	To tell
Dejar	To let, allow
Desear	To wish
Es aconsejable	It's advisable
Es importante	It's important
Es mejor	It's better
Es menester	It's necessary
Es necesario	It's necessary
Es preferible	It's preferable
Es prohibido	It's prohibited
Esperar	To hope
Hacer	To make
Insistir en	To insist on
Mandar	To command, order
Pedir	To request, order
Permitir	To permit
Preferir	To prefer
Prohibir	To prohibit, forbid
Querer	To want
Recomendar	To recommend
Rogar	To beg
Sugerir	To suggest
Suplicar	To beg, plead

*Now try these example sentences for verbs of **influence**. Take turns reading and translating to one another.*

Compañero(a) A:

1. Ella insiste en que nosotros hablemos en español.	1. She insists that we speak Spanish.
2. Es prohibido que Uds. entren por esta puerta.	2. It's prohibited that you all enter through this door.
3. Ellos esperan que nosotros disfrutemos el jardín.	3. They hope that we enjoy the garden.
4. Es necesario que Ud. haga ejercicio tres veces cada semana.	4. It's necessary that you exercise three times each week.
5. Ellos dicen que yo visite el museo nacional.	5. They tell me to visit the national museum.

Compañero(a) B:

1. Es importante que los pasajeros se sienten en los asientos rápidamente.	1. It's necessary that the passengers sit down in their seats quickly.
2. Mis padres me hacen que yo ayude en la casa.	2. My parents make me help in the house.
3. Espero que tú tengas cuidado.	3. I hope that you are careful.
4. Mando que tú pongas la mesa ahora.	4. I demand that you set the table now.
5. Te ruego que no vayas a ese lugar peligroso.	5. I beg you not to go to that dangerous place.

III. VERBS OF EMOTION

Alegrarse (de)	To be glad
Es bueno	It's good
Es fantástico, maravilloso, etc.	It's fantastic, marvelous, etc.
Es lástima	It's a pity
Es malo	It's bad
Es ridículo	It's ridiculous
Esperar	To hope
Estar contento(a)	To be happy
Ojalá	May God grant; Oh how I hope
Sentir	To regret

Sorprender	To be surprised
Temer	To fear
Tener miedo	To be afriad

*Now try these example sentences for verbs of **emotion**. Take turns reading and translating to one another.*

Compañero(a) A:

1. Me alegro de que tú sigas las instrucciones con cuidado.	1. I'm glad that you follow the directions carefully.
2. Es fantástico que Uds. estudien el español.	2. It's fantastic that you all are studying Spanish
3. Nosotros tememos que la niña esté perdida.	3. We fear that the little girl is lost.
4. Nos sorprende que tú no conozcas a Miguel.	4. It surprises us that you don't know Michael.
5. Ojalá que tú me acompañes a cenar.	5. Oh how I hope that you come with me to have dinner.

Compañero(a) B:

1. Espero que mis amigos me ayuden.	1. I hope that my friends help me.
2. Es una lástima que Uds. no se diviertan.	2. It's a pity/shame that you all aren't having fun.
3. Nos alegramos de que tú te sientas mejor.	3. We are glad that you feel better.
4. Siento que tú no puedas cenar conmigo esta noche.	4. I'm sorry that you can't eat dinner with me tonight.
5. Mi mamá está triste que yo sólo la llame de vez en cuando.	5. My mom is sad that I only call her once in a while.

III. PHRASES OF SPECULATION (The "unknown")

A menos	Unless
Antes de	Before
Así que	As soon as
Aunque	Although
Con tal (de)	Provided that
Cuando	When

De modo	So that
Después de	After
En caso de	In case of
En cuanto	As soon as
Hasta	Until
Mientras	While
Para	So, in order to, so that
Sin que	Without
Tan pronto como	As soon as

*Now try these example sentences for phrases of **speculation (the unknown antecedent)**. Take turns reading and translating to one another.*

Compañero(a) A:

1. Voy a llevar mi suéter en caso de que haga frío.	1. I am going to wear my sweater in case it's cold.
2. Leemos las frases ejemplares para que nuestros(as) compañeros(as) comprendan el subjuntivo.	2. We are reading the example sentences so that our partners will/might understand the subjunctive.
3. Te voy a llamar antes de que ellos lleguen.	3. I am going to call you before they arrive.
4. Ellos no van a cenar a menos que nosotros cenemos con ellos.	4. They aren't going to eat dinner unless we eat dinner with them.
5. Aunque pueda ser muy difícil, voy a estudiar el vocabulario cada noche.	5. Although it might be difficult, I am going to study the vocabulary every night.

Compañero(a) B:

1. Les escribo los ejemplos de modo que Uds. practiquen mucho.	1. I write the examples for you all so that you all might practice a lot.
2. Te doy el dinero cuando tú me des los boletos.	2. I'll give you the money when you give me the tickets.
3. No voy a salir hasta que Uds. lleguen.	3. I'm not going to leave/go out until you all arrive.

4. Ella salió sin que yo me despidiera de ella.	4. She left without me saying goodbye to her.
5. El banquero dice que va a darnos el préstamo tan pronto como llegue el estimado.	5. The banker says that he will give us the loan as soon as the estimate arrives.

*By now, you may have noticed that many of the subjunctive verbs in these sentences look a lot like the command form of the verb. The command form of a verb is like the subjunctive because a command is showing preference or desire over what someone else does just as the subjunctive does. The command is not an indicative tense because we don't know if the command will be carried out or performed. It's simply a request made by one person upon another. So, if you know and understand how to form the commands, you're halfway along the path to knowing how to conjugate verbs to the subjunctive! That's good news, right?!

*If the first verb (the trigger verb for the subjunctive) is in the present tense, the subjunctive verb will be in the present subjunctive. If the trigger verb is in the past tense, the subjunctive verb will be in the past subjunctive.

Ejemplos:

1. Ella quiere que nosotros estudiemos. = (*She wants us to study.*)

2. Ella quería que nosotros estudiáramos. = (*She wanted us to study.*)

3. Temo que los estudiantes no comprendan. = (*I fear that the students don't understand.*)

4. Yo temía que los estudiantes no comprendieran. = (*I feared that the students didn't understand.*)

5. La maestra no explica la lección hasta que los estudiantes la escuchen. = (*The teacher won't explain the lesson until the students listen to her.*)

6. La maestra nunca explicaba la lección hasta que los estudiantes la escucharan. = (*The teacher never used to explain the lesson until the students listened to her.*)

General rule for sequence of tenses:

Subject #1 + **Verb #1** + "que" + Subject #2 + **Verb #2** (S1V1 + que + S2**V2**)

When Verb #1 is in present tense, GENERALLY Verb #2 is in present subjunctive
When Verb #1 is in past tense, GENERALLY Verb #2 is in past (imperfect) subjunctive

How to conjugate verbs to the Present Subjunctive Mood

For regular verbs, there are three steps:

1. Find the "yo" form of the verb in the present tense

2. Drop the "o" of the yo form

3. Add the following endings to correspond to the subject:

For -AR Verbs   For -ER and -IR Verbs:

-e	-emos		-a	-amos
-es	-éis		-as	-áis
-e	-en		-a	-an

Práctica 7.2

Change the verb in parenthesis to the subjunctive. Then, take turns with your partner translating each sentence to English. Check with the back of the book if you're uncertain.

1. El jefe no quiere que sus empleados (usar) _____ sus teléfonos celulares en la oficina.

2. No me gusta que tú (trabajar) _____ hasta muy tarde por la noche.

3. Ojalá que Uds. (hacer) _____ todo el trabajo hoy.

4. Es importante que los empleados (seguir) _____ todas las instrucciones.

5. El jefe nos dice que nosotros (escribir) _____ los reportes ahora.

6. La compañía prohíbe que los clientes (ver) _____ los documentos de otros clientes.

7. Los empleados no hacen el trabajo hasta que el jefe se lo (mandar) _____.

8. Ellos quieren que nosotros (poner) _____ los documentos completos en los archivos.

9. Dudo que los clientes (tener) _____ tanto éxito con otra compañía.

10. Es importante que todos (conocer) _____ bien a su jefe y a sus empleados.

IRREGULAR VERBS IN THE PRESENT SUBJUNCTIVE

 ❖ –CAR, -GAR, -ZAR verbs (Verbs that end in –CAR, -GAR, or –ZAR)

 ❖ Verbs that ended in –CAR, -GAR, -ZAR will have a spelling change for all forms of the commands to maintain the sound of the infinitive ending. (Just like they did with the preterite tense)

–CAR		–GAR		–ZAR	
-que	-quemos	-gue	-guemos	-ce	-cemos
-ques	-quéis	-gues	-guéis	-ces	-céis
-que	-quen	-gue	-guen	-ce	-cen

Práctica 7.3
Change the verb in parenthesis to the subjunctive. Then, take turns with your partner translating each sentence to English. Check with the back of the book if you're uncertain.

1. Ojalá que Uds. (llegar) _____ a tiempo.

2. Dudamos que los empleados (almorzar) _____ en la cafetería.

3. No creo que el jefe (buscar) _____ los reportes.

4. Es preferido que tú (entregar) _____ los documentos temprano.

5. Los clientes esperan que Uds. (comenzar) _____ inmediatamente.

6. A los clientes les gusta cuando nosotros (tocar) _____ música.

❖ Remember the "Shoe" verbs? Just like when you were creating "nosotros" commands, note that any "nosotros" or "vosotros" subjunctive verb that ends with "-AR" or "-ER" will not have a stem change if it was a stem-changing verb in the present tense. All other forms of the subjunctive will.

Ejemplos:

contar = to count		mover = to move		entender = to understand	
Cuente	Contemos	Mueva	Movamos	Entienda	Entendamos
Cuentes	Contéis	Muevas	Mováis	Entiendas	Entendáis
Cuente	Cuenten	Mueva	Muevan	Entienda	Entiendan

❖ As it was with the "nosotros" command for verbs that ended with "-IR", there WILL be a stem change if it was a stem-changing verb in the present tense. "E" will change to "I", and "O" will change to "U" for the "nosotros" and "vosotros" forms of the subjunctive

Ejemplos:

morir = to die		dormir = to sleep		mentir = to liie	
Muera	Muramos	Duerma	Durmamos	Mienta	Mintamos
Mueras	Muráis	Duermas	Durmáis	Mientas	Mintáis
Muera	Mueran	Duerma	Duerman	Mienta	Mientan

Práctica 7.4
Change the verb in parenthesis to the subjunctive. Then, take turns with your partner translating each sentence to English. Check with the back of the book if you're uncertain.

1. Es importante que los empleados nunca (mentir) _____.

2. Ojalá que los clientes (entender) _____ las instrucciones.

3. Nuestro jefe prefiere que nosotros (empezar) _____ ahora.

4. Mi cliente quiere que yo (pedir) _____ su permiso antes de hacer decisiones importantes.

5. Mi colega y yo esperamos que el jefe (repetir) _____ las instrucciones.

6. Ojalá que mis colegas y yo no (reírse) _____ durante la presentación.

7. Es importante que todos los empleados (vestirse) _____ de ropa profesional.

Práctica 7.5

Study the picture below. Read the statements and decide if they are true (verdad) or false (falso) about what you see.

1. El chico quiere que la nadadora lo rescate.

2. El pescador espera que el chico no asuste a los peces.

3. En la playa se prohíbe que los perros entren en la playa.

4. Las reglas en la playa prohíben que los pescadores coman los peces.

5. Las personas que se sientan debajo de la sombrilla quieren que haga mucho sol.

6. Las personas debajo de la sombrilla quieren que el perro ladre (barks).

7. El chico quiere que el pescador lo vea.

8. El pescador quiere que el perro no ladre mucho.

❖ There are 5 irregular verbs

dar = to give			estar = to be			ir = to go	
Dé	Demos		Esté	Estemos		Vaya	Vayamos
Des	Deis		Estés	Estéis		Vayas	Vayáis
Dé	Den		Esté	Estén		Vaya	Vayan

saber = to know a fact			ser = to be	
Sepa	Sepamos		Sea	Seamos
Sepas	Sepáis		Seas	Seáis
Sepa	Sepan		Sea	Sean

Práctica 7.6
Decide which partner will read statements in Column A and which will read statements in Column B. Read the statements aloud to your partner, and have him/her tell you if they are true (verdad) or false (falso) about themselves or their beliefs.

A	B
1. Dudo que mis amigos vayan a la playa hoy.	1. Dudo que mis amigos me den un regalo hoy.
2. En mi opinión, es importante que los estudiantes sean amables.	2. En mi opinión, es importante que todos lleguen a clase a tiempo.
3. Mis amigos quieren que yo siempre esté contento(a).	3. Mis amigos quieren que yo siempre sepa todas las respuestas.
4. No creo que los maestros den demasiada tarea en las escuelas.	4. En general, no creo que los doctores sean amables.
5. Dudo que vaya a llover mucho este invierno.	5. Prefiero que nadie me dé regalos para mi cumpleaños.
6. Es mejor que los jóvenes no sepan nada de los asuntos financieros de la familia.	6. Es preferible que los jóvenes sepan manejar un coche con transmisión manual (caja de cambios).

Práctica 7.7

Study the picture below. Read the statements and decide if they are true (verdad) or false (falso) about what you see.

1. La mamá y el gato duermen en el sofá.
2. La mamá tiene un sueño malo.
3. La mamá quiere que las personas de su familia hagan los quehaceres de la casa.
4. La mamá espera que una persona de la familia lave los platos.
5. En su sueño, la mamá espera que una persona la lleve a la playa.
6. En su sueño, la mamá espera que una persona barra el suelo.
7. El gato quiere que la mamá trabaje más.
8. En realidad, la mamá duda que las otras personas vayan a ayudarla en la casa.
9. Es probable que la mamá haga todos los quehaceres de la casa.
10. Es evidente que la mamá siempre hace los quehaceres de la casa.
11. El gato también tiene un sueño.
12. El gato quiere que el perro se quede en su jaula (cage).

*Notice that there is no subjunctive used in sentence #10. This is because there is no doubt, uncertainty, influence or emotion expressed in the first clause. By stating that "it is evident" that the mom does the chores, there is no doubt - only certainty. No subjunctive is used if the speaker/writer is certain that the activity will (or won't) occur.

Práctica 7.8

You overhear parts of others' conversations. Where would you be when you hear them? Read the statements and decide which statements correspond to the location(s) listed. Some may take place in multiple locations. Discuss with your partner all answers that apply.

En un restaurante	En la oficina	En la primera cita (date)	En un hotel	En un banco
En un parque de atracciones	En el zoológico	En la playa durante las vacaciones	En el aeropuerto	En el avión
En la casa de un amigo	En una clase de español	En un partido de fútbol	En un concierto	En un museo

1. "Es importante que se quiten los zapatos antes de entrar."

2. "Espero que ellos acepten las tarjetas de crédito aquí."

3. "Dudo que el jugador vaya a hacer un gol."

4. "Es prohibido que nosotros toquemos las pinturas y esculturas."

5. "Es necesario que Uds. pongan el equipaje de mano en el portaequipaje."

6. "Recomiendo que lleves las sandalias en vez de los zapatos de tenis."

7. "Nos alegramos de que los animales estén contentos aquí."

8. "Ellos niegan que la montaña rusa sea peligrosa."

9. "Es necesario que Ud. nos muestre identificación."

10. "No estoy segura de que él pague la cuenta."

11. "Es mejor que no uses el diccionario."

12. "Es necesario que encontremos un cuarto con dos camas grandes."

13. "Recomiendo que hables con los clientes con mucha paciencia y cortesía."

14. "Me alegro de que sirvan comidas vegetarianas aquí."

15. "Les pido que Uds. formen una cola antes de abordar."

16. "Ojalá que toquen mi canción favorita."

17. "Ojalá que el tigre no se pueda escapar de su jaula."

18. "Te presento a mi familia cuando nos conozcamos mejor."

Chapter 8
Were You In the Mood?
Imperfect Subjunctive

Remember from the last chapter that the subjunctive is used in the following sentence patterns:

- ❖ Subject #1 + Verb #1 + "que" + Subject #2 + **Verb #2** (S1V1 + que + S2**V2**).
- ❖ Verb #1 is a "trigger verb" indicating Doubt, Influence, Emotion, or Speculation.
- ❖ Verb #2 is usually the verb in the subjunctive.
- ❖ When the trigger verb (verb #1) is in the present tense (or the future tense as we will learn in the next chapter), the subjunctive verb will be written in the present subjunctive.
- ❖ When the trigger verb (verb #1) is in the preterite, imperfect (or the conditional tense as we will learn in chapter 10), the subjunctive verb is written in the imperfect (or past) subjunctive

Take turns reading these examples aloud to your partner. Compare the tenses of each verb in the sentences:

Present tense ➜➜ present subjunctive	Past tense ➜➜ imperfect subjunctive
1. No creo que el subjuntivo sea difícil. *I don't believe the subjunctive is hard.*	1. Yo no creía que el subjuntivo fuera difícil. *I didn't believe the subjunctive was hard.*
2. Ella espera que Uds. lleguen a tiempo. *She hopes that you all arrive on time.*	2. Ella esperaba que Uds. llegaran a tiempo. *She hoped that you all arrived on time.*
3. La maestra nos dice que lo hagamos. *The teacher tells us to do it.*	3. La maestra nos dijo que lo hiciéramos. *The teacher told us to do it.*
4. Me alegro de que Uds. se diviertan. *I'm glad that you all are having fun.*	4. Me alegré de que Uds. se divirtieran. *I was glad that you all had fun.*
5. Es mejor que tú no vengas a la fiesta. *It is better that you don't come to the party.*	5. Fue mejor que tú no vinieras a la fiesta. *It was better that you didn't come to the party.*
6. Ellos no querrán que nosotros hablemos en inglés. *They will not want us to speak in English.* *"querrán" is written in the future tense	6. Ellos no querrían que nosotros habláramos en inglés. *They wouldn't want us to speak in English.* *"querrían" is the conditional tense

❖ To form the imperfect subjunctive, follow these steps:
1. Find the third person plural form (the "ellos", "ellas", "Uds." form) of the verb in the preterite tense.
2. Drop the ending "-ron"
3. Add the following ending to match the subject:

-ra	-´ramos
-ras	-rais
-ra	-ran

Práctica 8.1

Change the verb to the imperfect subjunctive by following the steps necessary to add the final endings.

Infinitive	3rd Person Plural Preterite	Imperfect Subjunctive
1. Vivir		Yo
2. Divertirse		Tú
3. Ser		Ud.
4. Ir		Él
5. Venir		Nosotros
6. Hacer		Vosotros
7. Sentarse		Ellos
8. Reírse		Uds.
9. Pagar		Yo
10. Dormir		Nosotros
11. Traer		Tú
12. Mentir		Ella

*NOTE: There is another set of endings that might be used. They are interchangeable with those listed above but are used less often. To keep things more simple, we will only be focusing on the most commonly used endings which are those listed above. Just for reference, below is the other set of endings you could add (or you might hear used, especially in Spain).

-se	-´semos
-ses	-seis
-se	-sen

Práctica 8.2

Change the verb in parenthesis to the past subjunctive. Then translate the sentence to English. Pay attention to the fact that these are all in the PAST tense now.

1. El seguridad quería que los pasajeros del avión (quitarse)

   _____ los zapatos antes de abordar el avión.

2. El entrevistador le preguntó al actor en una manera de que el actor no (poder)

   _____ mentir.

3. Yo te la expliqué para que tú (entender) _____ la situación.

4. Ellos no creían que nosotros (conocer) _____ al diplomático de ese país.

5. El intérprete habló lentamente para que nosotros (seguir)

   _____ escuchando la conversación.

6. Mi amiga esperaba que yo (traer) _____ las bebidas a su fiesta.

7. El jefe del negocio buscaba a una persona que (hablar) _____ español e inglés.

8. Mi novio no iba a ir a Aguascalientes a menos que yo (ir) _____ con él.

9. Yo no pude dormirme hasta que mi esposo (volver) _____.

10. Era dudoso que los estudiantes (estar) _____ contentos después de aprender las reglas del subjuntivo.

Práctica 8.3

Change the verb in parenthesis to the either the present or imperfect subjunctive, depending on the tense of the trigger verb. Then, take turns with your partner translating each sentence to English. Check with the back of the book for the answers if you're uncertain.

Remember the general rule for sequence of tenses as you do this exercise:

Main Clause (Indicative Tense) (Generally Verb #1)	Suborinate Clause (Subjunctive Verb) (Generally Verb #2)
Present Future	Present Subjunctive
Preterite Imperfect Conditional	Past (Imperfect) Subjunctive

1. Ellos no permitieron que nosotros (salir) _____ .

2. La maestra esperaba que los estudiantes (entender) _____ la lección.

3. Era probable que ellos (ver) _____ la película ayer.

4. Es probable que ella ya (saber) _____ las respuestas.

5. Me alegro de que Uds. (estar) _____ aquí esta noche.

6. Ella no creía que yo (ser) _____ presidente del club.

7. Yo dudo que él (pagar) _____ la cuenta.

8. Ella dudaba que él (conocer) _____ a Brad Pitt.

9. Uds. se alegran de que nosotros (hablar) _____ en español.

10. Es importante que nosotros (escuchar) _____ las instrucciones cuidadosamente.

11. Te recomendé que (ellos) (ir) _____ al Museo Nacional.

12. La maestra nos recomienda que (nosotros) (estudiar)

    _____ el vocabulario cada día.

13. Yo no creía que tú (querer) _____ hacer el trabajo.

14. Tú dudabas que yo (comer) _____ comida exótica.

Práctica 8.4

Think back to when you were a young teenager – around 13 or 14 years old. Answer the following questions about what your life was like at that age. Then, ask your partner the same questions and compare your responses.

Pregunta	Sobre mí	Sobre mi compañero/a
1. Insistían tus padres en que tú hicieras tu tarea inmediatamente después de volver de la escuela?		
2. ¿Querías que tus padres te dieran más libertad (freedom)?		
3. ¿Estudiaste sólo para que una universidad te aceptara?		
4. ¿Dudaste que las clases fueran importantes para tu futuro?		
5. ¿Era más importante que tú pasaras tiempo con amigos o con tu familia?		
6. ¿Te gustaba cuando tus amigos vinieran a tu casa o preferías que tus amigos te invitaran a sus casas?		
7. ¿Sugerían tus padres que tú participaras en actividades en la escuela?		
8. ¿Permitían tus padres que tú durmieras en las casas de tus amigos?		
9. ¿Salías de la casa sin que tus padres lo supieran?		
10. ¿Insistían tus amigos en que tú guardaras sus secretos?		

11. ¿Te aconsejaban tus padres que estudiaras más, que durmieras más, o que te divirtieras más?		
12. ¿Dudaste que tus amigos te dijeran siempre la verdad?		
13. ¿Preferías que tus padres te aconsejaran o que te dejaran hacer tus propias decisiones?		
14. ¿Tenías miedo de que nadie te gustara?		

Práctica 8.5

Read the story to your partner, asking questions along the way. Have your partner respond to the questions as you read. The answers are below the story for your reference.

Había un jefe muy desagradable. *(1. ¿Era el hombre jefe o empleado?)* El jefe se llamaba Jorge Gruñón. Era dueño de una revista muy popular. *(2. Era Jorge Gruñón dueño de un periódico o de una revista?)* El Sr. Gruñón siempre quería que sus empleados hicieran mucho trabajo. *(3. ¿Les dio el jefe mucho o poco trabajo a sus empleados?)* A los empleados no les molestaba que el jefe quería que hicieran mucho trabajo. Lo que les molestaba era que El Sr. Gruñón les pidió que hicieran trabajo sin importancia. *(4. ¿Tienen problemas los empleados con la idea de hacer mucho trabajo? ¿Era importante el trabajo que les dio el jefe?)*

Por ejemplo, un día el Sr. Gruñón llegó a la oficina y le pidió a Susana, una empleada muy talentosa, que ella le trajera café. *(5. Quería el jefe que Susana le trajera té o café?)* Pero él no quería café de la cafetera de la oficina. Claro que no. El Sr. Gruñón le mandó que Susana fuera a Starbucks para comprarle el café especial. Prefería el café de Starbucks porque creía que era más rico. *(6. Estaba contento el Sr. Gruñón con el café de la oficina? ¿Adónde quería que Susana fuera para comprar su café?)* Susana se graduó de la universidad y tenía un bachillerato en la fotografía. *(7. ¿Era Susana una empleada sin talento o con talento?)* Se graduó con honor de la universidad. Era fotógrafa y no le gustaba hacerle los recados de su jefe. *(8. ¿Aceptó Susana el trabajo de la revista para hacerle recados de su jefe o para sacar fotos?)* De todos modos, ella lo hizo porque quería ser fotógrafa para la revista.

Otro día el Sr. Gruñón le pidió a Pablo, un escritor maravilloso, que él llevara su ropa sucia a la lavandería. *(9. ¿Es Pablo mesero o escritor? ¿Quería el Sr. Gruñón que Pablo escribiera un artículo o que llevara su ropa a la lavandería?)* Pablo estaba enojado que el jefe le pidiera un mandado tan inútil, pero llevó la ropa a la lavandería.

(10. ¿Pablo escribió un artículo o llevó la ropa?) **Pablo creía que en el futuro, el jefe le iba a pedir que él escribiera un artículo para la revista.** *(11. Creía Pablo que iba a escribir un artículo en el futuro?)*

Y la pobre editora, Alisa... el Sr. Gruñón le pidió a ella que recogiera a sus hijos de la escuela. *(12. Tenía Alisa que recoger a sus propios hijos de la escuela o a los hijos del Sr. Gruñón?)* **Este mandado fue lo peor de todos porque los hijos del Sr. Gruñón, eran terribles. Siempre gritaban y le rogaban a Alisa que les comprara helado y otros dulces. Pero Alisa nunca se los compraba.** *(13. ¿Se portaban bien o mal los hijos del Sr. Gruñón? ¿Les compraba dulces Alisa?)*

La vida del Sr. Gruñón era buena, pero los empleados estaban tristes. *(14. Estaban contentos o enojados los empleados?)* **Pero un día, mientras Susana estaba en Starbucks, ella sacó una foto de un hombre. El hombre vio la foto, y le ofreció a Susana un trabajo con su revista.** *(15. ¿Quién sacó la foto? ¿Le gustó el hombre la foto? ¿Qué le ofreció a Susana? ¿Quería Susana trabajar para otra compañía?)* **Susana le dijo al hombre que ella conocía a dos empleados fantásticos – un escritor y una editora. Le pidió a su nuevo jefe que él les ofreciera trabajo.** *(16. ¿Quería Susana que su nuevo jefe les ofreciera más dinero o una posición con la compañía?)* **El hombre le dijo que prefería que sus fotógrafos trabajaran con personas de su preferencia. Así fue que los dos salieron juntos para hablar con Alisa y Pablo.** *(17. ¿Crees que Alisa y Pablo van a aceptar un trabajo con esta nueva revista?)*

Answers to questions that appear throughout Práctica 8.5:

1. empleado
2. dueño
3. mucho trabajo
4. no; no
5. café
6. no; a Starbucks
7. con talento
8. para sacar fotos
9. escritor; que llevara la ropa sucia a lavandería

10. llevó la ropa
11. sí
12. los hijos del Sr. Gruñón
13. se portaban mal; no les compraba dulces
14. estaban enojados
15. Susana; sí, le gustó; le ofreció trabajo; sí
16. una posición con la compañía
17. sí

Práctica 8.6
Now trade off! Change roles so the answering partner now reads this story, asking questions along the way. Have your partner respond to the questions as you read. The answers are below the story for your reference.

Había una vez una viajera que siempre viajaba por el mundo hispanohablante. *(1. ¿Viajó la mujer a países donde hablaban francés o español?)* **Ella se llamaba Carolina.** *(2. ¿Cómo se llamaba la viajera?)* **A Carolina le encantaba viajar, pero no era una**

viajera muy simpática.   Era una viajera grosera y egoísta. *(3. ¿Era Carolina simpática con otras personas de los otros países?)*

Por ejemplo, cuando Carolina estaba en otros países donde no hablaban inglés, ella insistía en que los nativos de ese país le hablaran en inglés. *(4. ¿Qué idioma hablaba Carolina? ¿Qué idioma quería Carolina que los nativos hablaran?)* Los nativos se enojaban generalmente, pero trataban de hablar en inglés para comunicarse con Carolina.   Los nativos no querían que Carolina estuviera descontenta con su visita. *(5. ¿Querían hablar inglés los nativos? ¿Querían que Carolina estuviera contenta? ¿En qué idioma hablaron los nativos con Carolina?)*

Un día mientras Carolina viajaba por México, ella decidió ir de compras en un mercado lleno de verduras frescas. *(6. ¿Quería comprar ropa o verduras Carolina?)* Ella quería comprar unos pimientos porque sabía que los pimientos de México eran muy ricos y únicos. *(7. ¿Quería comprar tomates o pimientos? ¿Quería pimientos porque son picantes o porque son ricos?)* Carolina empezó a hablar con una vendedora de pimientos. *(8. ¿Crees que Carolina habló con la vendedora en inglés o en español?)* Como de costumbre, Carolina empezó a hablar con la mujer en inglés.   La vendedora le contestó en español. *(9. ¿Quería Carolina que la vendedora hablara en inglés o en español?)* Carolina insistió en que la vendedora hablara en inglés, pero la vendedora no hablaba inglés.   Hablaba español. *(10. ¿Por qué hablaba español la vendedora - porque no quería o porque solo hablaba español?)* Carolina, le dijo a la vendedora, <<Me gustaría que me hablara en inglés. No voy a comprar nada a menos que me hable en inglés.>> *(11. Si la vendedora habla español, ¿va a comprar los pimientos Carolina? ¿Puede hablar inglés la vendedora?)* Y la mujer le respondió, <<No hablo inglés. Y estamos en México. Por favor, le suplico que me hable Ud. en español.>> *(12. ¿Quiere la vendedora que Carolina compre los pimientos de ella?)*

Carolina se enojó y le dijo a la mujer que no le gustó que la mujer no entendiera el inglés.   Carolina fue a la tienda que estaba inmediatamente a la derecha. *(13. ¿Adónde fue Carolina... a una tienda muy lejos o una tienda muy cerca?)* Esa vendedora oyó y vio todo entre Carolina y la otra mujer. *(14. ¿Escuchó la nueva vendedora la conversación entre Carolina y la otra vendedora?)* Carolina le dijo a la vendedora allí que ella compraría pimientos de ella si ella hablara en inglés. La otra vendedora se sonrió y le dijo que sí, le hablaría en inglés. *(15. ¿La vendedora de la tienda a la derecha entiende o no entiende el inglés?)*

Carolina le pidió en inglés que la mujer le diera unos pimientos muy ricos y únicos – los más ricos y únicos de todos. *(16. ¿Pidió Carolina los pimientos frescos y dulces o ricos y únicos?)* La vendedora le sonrió y le dio una bolsa llena de pimientos.

En inglés, la vendedora le dijo a Carolina, <<Escogí los pimientos mejores para Ud..>> *(17. ¿Escogió Carolina los pimientos?)*

Carolina caminó al parque para comer unos de los pimientos. *(18. ¿Por qué fue Carolina al parque... para leer o para comer?)* Cuando llegó allí, se sentó en un banco, y abrió la bolsa. Se sorprendió que la mujer hubiera puesto solamente pimientos viejos y podridos (rotten) en la bolsa. *(19. ¿Escogió pimientos buenos o malos la vendedora?)* Había sólo un pimiento bueno en la bolsa. *(20. ¿Estaban todos los pimientos malos?)* Carolina lo sacó y tomó un bocadillo. *(21. ¿Comió Carolina una parte o no comió ninguna parte del pimiento?)* ¡Era tan picante que se sintió como hubiera un fuego en su boca! No pudo comer ni un bocadillo más. *(22. ¿Pudo comer el pimiento Carolina? ¿Crees que la vendedora escogió el pimiento más picante? ¿Quería la vendedora enseñarle a Carolina una lección?)* De ahí en adelante, Carolina no insistió en que otras personas hablaran en inglés. *(23. ¿Aprendió Carolina una lección de esta experiencia?)* Ella decidió tomar clases de español para hablar con las personas en español. *(24. Como resultado de su experiencia, ¿qué va a hacer Carolina?)*

Answers to questions that appear throughout Práctica 8.6:

1. español
2. Carolina
3. no
4. inglés; inglés
5. no; sí; inglés
6. verduras
7. pimientos; porque son ricos
8. inglés
9. inglés
10. solo hablaba español
11. no; no
12. sí

13. una tienda cerca
14. sí
15. entiende inglés
16. ricos y únicos
17. no
18. para comer
19. malos
20. no
21. comió una parte
22. no; sí
23. sí
24. aprender el español

Práctica 8.7

While waiting for your plane to take off, you saw the following scene. You thought it was amusing, so you took a photo. Now you're back home and you're showing friends this photo. They want to know what was going on. Answer the questions your friends ask you. Use the answers on the next page and choose the best one to answer your friends' questions.

1. ¿Por qué estaba enojada la mamá de la joven?
2. ¿Por qué no se le sonrió la joven a su mamá?
3. ¿Qué quería el niño que agarraba la falda de su mamá?
4. ¿Qué quería la mamá del niño?
5. ¿Por qué tenía la empleada un micrófono en la mano?
6. ¿Por qué miraba los relojes el hombre con la maleta?
7. ¿Por qué estaba de mal humor el hombre con el teléfono celular?
8. ¿Por qué se sonreía la empleada mientras todos los pasajeros se quejaban y se enojaban?

Quería que su esposa contestara el teléfono para que pudiera hablar con ella.	Quería que su mamá lo llevara al baño.
Quería que la gente formaran una cola para abordar el avión.	Sabía que todos iban a salir dentro de poco tiempo.
La mamá no estaba contenta de que su hija siempre usara su teléfono celular en vez de hablar con ella.	Quería que la empleada de la línea aérea le diera su tarjeta de embarque.
No quería levantarse para que su mamá pudiera sentarse en la silla al lado de ella.	No creía que su avión llegara tarde porque no sabía qué hora era.

Chapter 9
What Have YOU Done?
The Present Perfect Tense

The present perfect tense expresses an action that someone "has done" or "hasn't done" in the past.

The present perfect usually describes an action that began in the past and still continues into the present. Or the present perfect describes a past action that somehow connects to a present action or situation.

Because the past action relates to a present one, the present perfect often is accompanied by the words "**ya**" (already), as in "*I have already…*" or "**todavía**" (still) as in "*She still hasn't …*"

Read the following examples of sentences that use the present tense:

Spanish	English
1. Yo *he hablado* con la profesora.	1. I have spoken with the teacher.
2. Ella ya *ha comido*.	2. She has already eaten.
3. ¿Todavía no *has escrito* esa carta?	3. You still haven't written that letter?
4. Los estudiantes ya *han leído* ese capítulo.	4. The students have already read that chapter.
5. Nosotros no *hemos recomendado* nada.	5. We haven't recommended anything.
6. ¿*Habéis estudiado* para el examen?	6. Have you guys studied for the test?

❖ The perfect tense is a compound tense meaning that we use two verbs together to form the tense.
❖ The first verb is a conjugated form of the verb "**haber**" which means, "to have" as in someone "has done" or "hasn't done" an activity. Be careful not to confuse "tener" (to have) with "haber" (to have). The verb "haber" is an auxiliary verb and is the only "to have" we can use with the perfect tenses.
❖ We use the present tense conjugation of the verb "haber" to form the present perfect.

Here are the present tense conjugations of the verb "haber"

I have	He	We have	Hemos
You have	Has	You guys have	Habéis
You (formal) have He has She has It has	Ha	You all have They have	Han

❖ The second verb used to form the present perfect tense is a past participle.
❖ To form a **past participle**:
    1. Drop the ending of the verb infinitive
    2. Add " **–ado** " for "- AR" verbs or "**–ido**" for –ER and –IR verbs

Prática 9.1

Change these verbs to past participles and translate the participle to English.

Verb Infinitive	Past Participle	English Translation
Hablar		
Vivir		
Almorzar		
Entender		
Conocer		
Aburrir		
Cerrar		
Preocupar		

❖ *Nota: Past participles may also be used as adjectives; for example, "La puerta está cerrada." to mean "The door is closed." or, "Nosotros estamos muy preocupados." to say "We are worried." When the past participle is used as an adjective, it does not use the verb "haber" before it. Also, when they are used as adjectives they must match in gender and number with the noun they modify.

❖ The participles, when used with "haber" to form the perfect tenses do not change in gender. When used with the perfect tenses, the ending of the past participle always ends in "o".

❖ Verbs that end in -ER or –IR and have a vowel right before, require an accent mark to be placed over the "i".

Infinitive	Past Participle	English Translation
Caer	Caído	Fallen
Creer	Creído	Believed
Leer	Leído	Read
Oír	Oído	Heard
Reír	Reído	Laughed
traer	Traído	Brought

Irregular Past Participles

Infinitive	Past Participle	English Translation
Abrir	Abierto	Opened
Cubrir	Cubierto	Covered
Decir	Dicho	Said, told
Escribir	Escrito	Written
Freír	Frito	Fried

Hacer	Hecho	Made, done
Morir	Muerto	Died
Poner	Puesto	Put, placed
Resolver	Resuelto	Resolved
Romper	Roto	Broken
Ver	Visto	Seen
Volver	Vuelto	Returned

Práctica 9.2

Now, let's put the conjugation of haber and the past participle together to translate these sentences:

1. She has recommended the Mexican restaurant.

_____

_____

2. We have learned a lot in this class! ☺

_____

_____

3. Have you guys seen the movie "Macario"?

_____

4. I haven't brought my book today.

_____

5. You guys have done the work!

_____

6. Carlos, you have heard the news, right?

_____

7. I haven't traveled there for years.

_____

_____

8. Have you studied for the test, Susana?

_____

9. My friends have seen me.

_____

10. Miguel and Rafael have laughed all night.

_____

_____

11. Who has told you that lie?

_____

_____

12. You guys haven't written the letter?

_____

_____

Práctica 9.3

Tell your partner who you know who has done the following activities. Change the infinitive to the present perfect to match the person who did the activity.
Ejemplo: subir la torre Eiffel ➔   *Mi familia y yo hemos subido la torre Eiffel.*

1. viajar a Costa Rica

_____

2. escribir una novela

_____

3. rescatar a un animal

_____

4. salvar la vida de una persona

_____

5. pintar un autorretrato (self-portrait)

_____

6. hacer una blusa o vestido

_____

7. plantar un jardín de verduras

_____

8. diseñar (to design) una casa o un edificio

_____

9. tener cirugía (surgery)

_____

10. correr un maratón

_____

Práctica 9.4

Read the following story aloud with your partner in volleyball style! Have Student A read the first sentence in Spanish. Then, Student B translates that first sentence to English and reads the next sentence aloud in Spanish. Student A translates to English the sentence just read and then reads the next in English. Students alternate reading and translating until you reach the end of the story.

Mis amigos y yo hemos hecho muchas actividades este verano. Hemos viajado por avión desde Nueva York hasta California. Hemos pasado unos días en San Francisco. Hemos visitado a unos familiares de mi amiga, Katia. Ya hemos pasado unos días en el sur de California en Los Ángeles. Dos de nuestro grupo han visitado El Museo de Tolerancia. Yo no fui con ellos, pero yo he ido al Museo de Historia Natural. Aquí en Los Ángeles he visto muchos lugares interesantes. He visto a la gente vendiendo cosas raras en la playa de Venice. He visto el muelle de Santa Mónica con todas las atracciones y tiendas de comida. Pero también he hecho unas actividades maravillosas aquí. Por ejemplo, mis amigos y yo hemos patinado por el sendero que va por todas las playas. Hemos tomado un tour en un autobús de dos pisos. Hemos puesto nuestras manos en las impresiones de manos de los actores famosos de Hollywood. También hemos buscado a las estrellas de Hollywood, pero todavía no hemos visto a ningún actor famoso. ¿Has visto tú a unas personas famosas en Hollywood?

Práctica 9.5

Look at the pictures below. Match the name(s) with the person(s) who has/have done the activity.

1. ¿Quién(es) ha(n) subido la torre Eiffel?
2. ¿Quién(es) ha(n) tenido unas aventuras divertidas?
3. ¿Quién(es) ha(n) corrido con los toros?
4. ¿Quién(es) ha(n) escalado una montaña?
5. ¿Quién(es) ha(n) viajado a España?
6. ¿Quién(es) ha(n) viajado por Sudamérica por autobús?
7. ¿Quién(es) ha(n) tenido miedo en su viaje?
8. ¿Quién(es) ha(n) viajado a un lugar donde hacía frío?

Look at the pictures below. Match the name(s) with the person(s) who has/have done the activity listed on the next page.

1. ¿Quién(es) ha(n) trabajado hoy?
2. ¿Quién(es) ha(n) depositado dinero en el banco hoy?
3. ¿Quién(es) ha(n) enseñado una clase hoy?
4. ¿Quién(es) ha(n) pasado tiempo con amigos hoy?
5. ¿Quién(es) se ha(n) sentido frustrado/a hoy?
6. ¿Quién(es) ha(n) salido de la casa hoy?
7. ¿Quién(es) ha(n) ido de compras hoy?
8. ¿Quién(es) ha(n) dibujado hoy?
9. ¿Quién(es) se ha(n) divertido más hoy?
10. ¿Quién(es) ha(n) gastado demasiado dinero hoy?

Chapter 10
What You Had Done
The Pluperfect Tense

The pluperfect tense is also known as the past perfect tense. The pluperfect tense expresses an action that someone "had done" or "hadn't done" in the past.

The pluperfect tense usually describes an action that was completed in the past before another action started.

The pluperfect often, but not always, is accompanied by the following words:

Spanish	English
Cuando	When
Después de que	After
Tan pronto como	As soon as
Apenas	Scarcely, hardly
Ya	Already

Read the following examples of sentences that use the pluperfect tense:

Spanish	English
1. Ya yo *había hablado* con la profesora cuando los estudiantes llegaron.	1. I had already spoken with the teacher when the students arrived.
2. Ella apenas *había comido* el plato principal cuando el mesero le trajo el postre.	2. She had scarcely eaten the main course when the waiter brought her the dessert.
3. ¿Todavía no *habías escrito* esa carta?	3. You still hadn't written that letter?
4. Los estudiantes ya *habían leído* ese capítulo.	4. The students had already read that chapter.
5. Nosotros no *habíamos recomendado* nada.	5. We hadn't recommended anything.
6. ¿*Habíais estudiado* para el examen?	6. Had you guys studied for the test?

❖ The pluperfect tense is a compound tense meaning that we use two verbs together to form the tense.
❖ The first verb is a conjugated form of the verb "**haber**" which means "to have" as in someone "had done" or "hadn't done" an activity.

- ❖ We use the imperfect tense conjugation of the verb "haber" to form the present perfect.

Here are the imperfect tense conjugations of the verb "haber" I have

I had	**Había**	We had	**Habíamos**
You had	**Habías**	You guys had	**Habíais**
You (formal) had He had She had It had	**Había**	You all had They had	**Habían**

Práctica 10.1

Translate the following sentences to Spanish.

1. Who had read this chapter before entering class?

_____

_____

2. We had barely opened the door when they called.

_____

_____

3. As soon as we had arrived, our friends left.

_____

_____

4. I hadn't seen that movie.

_____

5. My friends had put the books in my car.

_____

6. Anita, had you closed the windows before it started to rain?

_____

_____

7. Had you guys opened the doors?

_____

_____

8. Had you all sung the song?

_____

Práctica 10.2

Put a checkmark next to the activities that you had done before starting this activity today. Then, compare your answers to your partner's by asking if he/she had done these activities.

_____ Había visto las noticias en la televisión.

_____ Había hablado con mis parientes.

_____ Me había cepillado los dientes.

_____ Había preparado mi almuerzo para mañana.

_____ Había tomado café.

_____ Había pasado tiempo con amigos.

_____ Había conducido un carro.

_____ Había escuchado música en el radio.

_____ Había pagado unas facturas (bills).

_____ Había hablado por teléfono con unos amigos.

_____ Había comprado algo nuevo.

_____ Había ido de compras en una tienda de ropa.

_____ Había comprado comida del supermercado.

_____ Había leído unos capítulos de una novela.

_____ Había mandado un "text".

_____ Había estudiado español.

_____ Había hablado en español con una persona hispanohablante.

_____ Había organizado mi casa.

Práctica 10.3

Look at the picture below and discuss the answers to the questions with your partner. Use the bank of words below to help you answer the questions.

The woman – la mujer	Outside - afuera	The tree – el árbol
The daughter – la hija	Inside - adentro	The kitchen – la cocina
The man – el hombre	The ballet shoes – las zapatillas de ballet	The meal – la comida
The parents – los padres	The suit – el traje	The salt and pepper – la sal y la pimienta

1. ¿Quiénes son las personas en el dibujo? ¿Crees que son parte de la misma familia?
2. ¿Qué había hecho la hija? ¿Cómo sabes?
3. ¿Qué había hecho el hombre? ¿Cómo sabes?
4. ¿Qué había hecho la mujer? ¿Cómo sabes?
5. ¿Había salido del trabajo o va a salir para el trabajo el hombre?
6. ¿Crees que la hija se había divertido? ¿Cómo sabes?
7. ¿Le había gustado el trabajo el hombre? ¿Cómo sabes?
8. ¿Había comprado o preparado la comida la mujer?

Práctica 10.4

Study the picture sequence below. Tell what Sofía had done to bake the birthday cake for her son. List as many steps as you can! Use the bank of words on the next page to help you.

Ejemplo: "Ella había ido al mercado para comprar los ingredientes." = She had gone to the store to buy the ingredients.

The cake = el pastel (o) la torta	The birthday cake = el pastel de cumpleaños	The recipe = la receta	The cake mix = el polvo para hacer pastel
To mix = mezclar	The flour = la harina	The ingredients = los ingredientes	The oven = el horno
The bowl = el recipiente	The sugar = el azúcar	To bake = hornear	The cake pan = la bizcochera
To take out = sacar	To frost the cake = cubrir el pastel de escarcha	The candles = las velas	To light = encender
To measure = medir	The basket = la cesta	The measuring cup = la taza para medir	Measuring spoons = las cucharas para medir
The party hat = el sombrero de fiesta	The apron = el delantal	Degrees = grados	The spatula = la espátula
The baking soda = el bicarbonato	The egg = el huevo	The oil = el aceite	The baking powder = la levadura en polvo
To cool = enfriar	To heat = calentar	To add = añadir	To serve = servir

1. _____

2. _____

3. _____

4. _____

5. _____

6. _____

7. _____

8. _____

9. _____

10. _____

Chapter 11
What's in The Crystal Ball?
The Future Tense

So far you've learned to talk about the future by using the expression "ir + a + infinitive" as in "Voy a comer" to mean "I am going to eat." Or, "Uds. van a hablar en español." meaning "You all are going to speak in Spanish."

Though this expression works well to express what is going to happen, there is a true future tense in Spanish that expresses what "will happen", or indicates that someone is wondering about what will happen in the future.

Read these examples with your partner and see if you can find a pattern to forming the future tense.

Spanish	English
1. Nosotros hablaremos en español hoy.	1. We will speak Spanish today.
2. Los empleados escribirán los documentos.	2. The employees will write the documents.
3. ¿Escucharás tú las noticias esta noche?	3. Will you listen to the news tonight?
4. Vosotros iréis a España este verano, ¿no?	4. You guys will go to Spain this summer, right?
5. Yo jugaré al fútbol este fin de semana.	5. I will play soccer this weekend.
6. Miguel será abogado en el futuro.	6. Miguel will be a lawyer in the future.
7. ¿Cuántas personas habrá en la fiesta?	7. (I wonder) how many people there will be at the party?

To form the future tense in Spanish
   ❖ Add the following endings to the INFINITIVE of the verb:

Yo	**– é**	Nosotros(as)	**– emos**
Tú	**– ás**	Vosotros(as)	**– éis**
Ud. Él Ella	**– á**	Uds. Ellos Ellas	**– án**

Práctica 11.1

Fill in the verb with the future tense. Then, translate the sentences to English.

1. El jefe (requerir) _____ que los empleados completen el trabajo.

_____

_____

2. Yo (pagar) _____ la cuenta.

_____

_____

3. Los estudiantes (asistir) _____ a las clases.

_____

_____

4. ¿(Estar) _____ Uds. contentos?

_____

5. ¿(Vender) _____ vosotros los carros viejos?

_____

6. Mis amigos y yo (sentarse) _____ en la primera fila en la clase.

_____

7. El doctor (leer) _____ los resultados.

_____

8. ¿(Traer) _____ tú las empanadas?

_____

9. (Ser) _____ la una de la tarde cuando lleguen.

_____

10. Tú y yo (conocer) _____ a nuevos amigos.

_____

Irregular Verbs in the Future Tense

❖ The irregular verbs in the future are irregular only in that they change their stem. The endings of the verbs work just like the regular verbs do.

❖ To form the irregular verbs, use the stem listed below for the verb and add the regular future tense endings.

Verb in English	Infinitive of Spanish Verb	Stem of Future Tense
To fit	Caber	Cabr-
To say, tell	Decir	Dir-
There will be; to have	Haber	Habr-
To do, make	Hacer	Har-
To be able to, can	Poder	Podr-
To put, to place	Poner	Pondr-
To want, like, love	Querer	Querr-
To know (a fact, how to)	Saber	Sabr-
To leave, go out	Salir	Saldr-
To have	Tener	Tendr-
To be worth	Valer	Valdr-
To come	Venir	Vendr-

Ejemplos:

1. Yo siempre diré la verdad = *I will always tell the truth.*
2. Ella pondrá los documentos en el archivo. = *She will put the documents in the folder.*
3. Haremos el trabajo mañana. = *We will do the work tomorrow.*

131

4. ¿Quién sabrá la respuesta? = *(I wonder) who will know the answer?*

5. Mis parientes vendrán la semana entrante. = *My realtives will come next week.*

6. ¿Qué habrá en ese cuarto? = *(I wonder) what will there be in that room?*

7. ¿Cuándo saldremos? = *When will we leave?*

8. No entraremos en esa tienda porque los niños querrán dulces. = *We will not enter in that store because the little kids will want sweets/candy.*

Práctica 11.2
Fill in the verb with the future tense. Then, translate the sentences to English.

1. Yo (haber) _____ leído capítulo dos para la próxima clase.

_____

_____

2. Nosotros (querer) _____ practicar más.

_____

3. Ana (salir) _____ a las ocho de la mañana.

_____

4. (Haber) _____ muchos documentos para firmar.

_____

5. Esa escultura (valer) _____ mucho dinero.

_____

6. Creo que esos libros (caber) _____ en el estante para libros.

_____

_____

7. Uds. (haber) _____ escrito muchas de las palabras.

_____

_____

8. Mi familia (poder) _____ ir con Uds. al lago.

_____

9. Yo no (saber) _____ jugar pero yo (poder) _____ mirar el partido.

_____

_____

10. ¿(Tener) _____ tú ganas de ir de compras mañana?

_____

_____

Práctica 11.3

Below are some goals or resolutions for the new year. Put a checkmark in the column "metas para mí" if they are goals you plan to meet in the future. Then, ask your partner if he/she plans to meet these goals in his/her future. Put a checkmark in the column "metas para mi compañero/a" if he/she plans to meet that goal.

Metas (Goals)	Metas para mí	Metas para mi compañero/a
1. Tendré más paciencia con otros.		
2. Perderé de peso.		
3. Haré más ejercicio.		
4. Ganaré de peso.		
5. Comeré comida más saludable.		
6. Pasaré más tiempo con mi familia y amigos.		
7. Ahorraré dinero.		
8. Trabajaré más.		
9. Viajaré a otro país.		
10. Buscaré empleo nuevo.		

Práctica 11.4

Study the following picture. Then, answer the questions that follow. Use the vocabulary in the bank of words below to help you.

The fortune teller = la adivina	The crystal ball = la bola de cristal	The turban = el turbante
The cruise = el crucero	The ring = el anillo	To propose = proponer
To get married = casarse	The future = el futuro	The bells = las campanas
The ship = el barco	To happen = pasar	To charge = cobrar

1. ¿Quiénes son las personas en el dibujo? ¿Cómo sabes?
2. ¿Por qué vino la mujer a hablar con la adivina?
3. ¿Qué indica el anillo en la bola de cristal?
4. ¿Qué dirá la adivina del futuro de la mujer?
5. ¿Crees que el futuro de la mujer será buena o mala? ¿Por qué?
6. ¿Estará contenta la mujer con la predicción?
7. ¿Qué representan el barco y el coche?
8. ¿Por qué hay cartas en la mesa?

Práctica 11.5

What are some of your plans for this upcoming weekend and week? Write five activities you plan to do and share them with your partner.

1. _____

2. _____

3. _____

4. _____

5. _____

Práctica 11.6

Be a fortune teller yourself. Make predictions about what each of the following people will do five years from now.

1. Mi mejor amigo/a... _____

_____

2. Mi pariente, _____, ... _____

_____

3. Mi compañero/a ..._____

_____

4. Mi maestra de español... _____

_____

5. Yo .... _____

_____

Práctica 11.7

Look at the picture. Discuss the answers to the questions that follow with your partner.

1. ¿Es una ceremonia de matrimonio o de graduación?
2. ¿Piensa la joven en el pasado o en el futuro?
3. ¿Será una estudiante de la escuela secundaria o de la universidad?
4. ¿Piensa la mujer en las profesiones que tendrá o en las amigas que conoció en la universidad?
5. En la imaginación de la joven, ¿será astronauta o física?
6. ¿Quizás será veterinaria o pediatra?
7. ¿Será maestra o conductora de autobús?
8. ¿Cree la joven que tendrá éxito en el futuro?

Chapter 12
What WOULD YOU Do?
The Conditional Tense

The conditional tense is used to express what "would happen" or "wouldn't happen" (usually under certain circumstances). It is used to show what someone "would do" or "wouldn't do".

Ejemplos:
1. Carolina no hablaría en español. = *Carolina wouldn't speak in Spanish.*
2. Yo leería las instrucciones antes de comenzar la actividad. = *I would read the instructions before beginning the activity.*
3. Nosotros estudiaríamos antes del examen. = *We would study before the test.*
4. ¿Viajarías a España? = *Would you travel to Spain?*
5. Les gustaría ir al cine. = *They would like to go to the movies.*

❖ One common mistake Spanish language learners make is to confuse the conditional with the imperfect tense. Both translate in English as "would do something". But notice the difference between these examples.

Imperfect	Conditional
1. Ella comía en restaurantes mexicanos. *She would (used to) eat in Mexican restaurants.*	1. Ella comería en restaurantes mexicanos. *She would (if given the opportuinity) eat in Mexican restaurants.*
2. Yo siempre leía todo antes de firmar. *I would always read everything before signing.*	2. Yo leería todo antes de firmar. *I would read everything before signing (if I were you).*
3. Los estudiantes estudiaban. *The students would (always) study.*	3. Los estudiantes estudiarían. *The students would study (if they could).*
4. El jugador hacía todos los goles. *The player would score all the goals (it always happened).*	4. El jugador haría los goles. *The player would score goals (in a future game, if he could).*

❖ The imperfect examples indicate the action would (or wouldn't) happen continually in the past. The conditional examples indicate that an action would (or wouldn't) happen under different or specific circumstances.

To form the conditional tense in Spanish

Add the following endings to the INFINITIVE of the verb:

Yo	**- ía**	Nosotros(as)	**- íamos**
Tú	**- ías**	Vosotros(as)	**- íais**
Ud. Él ella	**- ía**	Uds. Ellos ellas	**- ían**

Práctica 12.1

Fill in the verb with the condtional tense. Then, translate the sentences to English.

1. El jefe (requerir) _____ que los empleados completaran el trabajo.

_____

_____

2. Si fuéramos al restaurante, yo (pagar) _____ la cuenta.

_____

_____

3. Si las clases ocurrieran los jueves, los estudiantes (asistir).

_____

_____

4. ¿(Estar) _____ Uds. contentos si nosotros les diéramos más tarea?

_____

_____

5. ¿ (Vender) _____ vosotros los carros viejos?

_____

6. Mis amigos y yo (sentarse) _____ en la primera
fila en la clase, pero los otros estudiantes estaban allí.

_____

_____

7. El doctor (leer) _____ los resultados, pero el paciente
no estuvo allí.

_____

_____

8. ¿(Traer) _____ tú las empanadas?

_____

9. (Ser) _____ la una de la tarde cuando llegaron.

_____

10. Tú y yo (conocer) _____ a nuevos amigos si fuéramos a
la fiesta.

_____

_____

11. Yo no (hacer) _____ eso si yo fuera tú.

_____

12. (Nevar) _____ si hiciera más frío.

_____

Irregular Verbs in the Conditional Tense

❖ The irregular verbs in the conditional tense are irregular only in that they change their stem. The endings of the verbs work just like the regular verbs do.

❖ To form the irregular verbs, use the stem listed below for the verb and add the regular endings.

Verb in English	Infinitive of Spanish Verb	Stem of Future Tense
To fit	Caber	Cabr-
To say, tell	Decir	Dir-
There will be; to have	Haber	Habr-
To do, make	Hacer	Har-
To be able to, can	Poder	Podr-
To put, to place	Poner	Pondr-
To want, like, love	Querer	Querr-
To know (a fact, how to)	Saber	Sabr-
To leave, go out	Salir	Saldr-
To have	Tener	Tendr-
To be worth	Valer	Valdr-
To come	Venir	Vendr-

Ejemplos:

1. Yo le diría la verdad = *I would tell him the truth.*
2. Ella pondría los documentos en el archivo. = *She would put the documents in the folder.*
3. Haríamos el trabajo mañana. = *We would do the work tomorrow.*
4. ¿Quién sabría la respuesta? = *Who would know the answer?*
5. Mis parientes vendrían la semana entrante, pero mi primo estaba enfermo. = *My realtives would come next week, but my cousin was sick.*
6. ¿Qué habría en ese cuarto? = *I wonder what could there be in that room?*
7. ¿Cuándo saldríamos? = *When would we leave?*
8. No entraríamos en esa tienda porque los niños querrían dulces. = *We would not enter in that store because the little kids would want sweets/candy.*

Práctica 12.2

Fill in the verb with the conditional tense. Then, translate the sentences to English.

1. Yo (haber) _____ leído capítulo dos, pero yo no tenía tiempo.

_____

_____

2. Nosotros (querer) _____ practicar más.

_____

3. Ana (salir) _____ a las ocho para llegar a tiempo.

_____

_____

4. (Haber) _____ muchos documentos para firmar.

_____

5. Esa escultura (valer) _____ mucho dinero si pudiéramos comprarla.

_____

_____

6. Creía que esos libros (caber) _____ en el estante para libros.

_____

_____

7. Uds. (haber) _____ escrito muchas de las palabras.

_____

8. Yo creía que mi familia (poder) _____ ir con Uds. al lago.

_____

_____

9. Yo no (saber) _____ jugar porque nunca (haber) _____
   jugado antes.

_____

_____

10. ¿(Tener) _____ tú ganas de ir de compras mañana?

_____

_____

11. ¿(Venir) _____ sus primos con nosotros?

_____

12. ¿Quiénes (haber) _____ hecho reservaciones para
nosotros?

_____

_____

13. ¿Le (decir) _____ tú mi secreto a Marta?

_____

_____

14. Si tu novia viniera a cenar, ¿qué (querer) _____ ella
para comer?

_____

_____

Práctica 12.3

Study the following picture. Then, answer the questions that follow. Use the vocabulary from the bank of words below to help you.

The travel agent – el/la agente de viajes	The poster – el cartel	The country – el país
To relax - relajarse	The rain forest – el bosque tropical	The fortress – la fortaleza
To sightsee – hacer turismo	The sand on the beach – la arena de la playa	To sunbathe –tomar el sol
The tree frog – el coquí	To show – mostrar/enseñar	To recommend - recomendar

1. ¿Quién es la persona en el dibujo?
2. Según la agente de viajes, ¿adónde viajaría?
3. ¿Qué vería una persona en Puerto Rico?
4. ¿Tomaría el sol en Puerto Rico?
5. En un viaje a Puerto Rico, ¿dónde encontrarías el coquí?
6. Según el cartel, ¿adónde irías para aprender un poco de la historia de Puerto Rico?
7. ¿Hay mucho o poco para hacer turismo en Puerto Rico?
8. ¿Hablarías tú con agente de viajes para buscar información sobre Puerto Rico?

Chapter 13
Look What You Can Do!
Mastery Exercises

Práctica 13.1
Read the following autobiography by the author. Then, using similar information write your own autobiography. Just as this example does, include the following information:

1. Where and when were you born?
2. Tell about your parents and childhood family.
3. Tell what your childhood was like.
4. Tell about at least one significant life-changing event.
5. Briefly tell of your schooling or any experience leading to your job.
6. Say at least a few of your favorites – things you like to do, things you like and don't like. Provide details or examples.
7. Express at least one or two activities you'd like to do in the future.

Me llamo Melissa. Nací en Glendale, California al fin de los años sesenta. En mi familia hay mis padres, mis dos hermanos mayores y yo. Mi padre era abogado y muy trabajador. Mi mamá era ama de casa y siempre nos cuidaba. Me gustaba mucho pasar tiempo con mi familia. Generalmente, mi familia y yo íbamos a un lago en las montañas para pasar los fines de semana. Me encantaba pescar, andar en mi bicicleta, o montar una motocicleta con mi hermano. También durante los veranos, me gustaba hacer el esquí acuático. Yo era una joven muy activa y pasaba mucho tiempo fuera de la casa. Pero mi actividad favorita era patinar sobre hielo. Yo patinaba tres veces cada semana y a veces competía en competencias locales.

Era una estudiante muy buena y mi materia favorita era la literatura. Cuando tenía dieciséis años, yo viajé al Perú como estudiante de un programa de intercambio. Allí, aprendí mucho sobre la gente y la cultura peruana. Me fascinó la cultura y me enamoré de la gente tan simpática y buena allí. A causa de esta experiencia, estudié español y literatura en la universidad. Viví y estudié en México. Me gradué y me hice maestra de un colegio en mi comunidad nativa.

Todavía me encanta el idioma español y la gente hispanoblante. Me encanta viajar, pero no me gusta viajar por avión. Tengo miedo de volar por avión. Mi esposo maravilloso, nuestros hijos y yo pasamos mucho tiempo juntos. Me gustan mucho los perros y tengo dos en mi casa. Cada día camino con ellas.

Me gustaría viajar más en el futuro. Algún día viajaré a España con mi familia. Ojalá que pueda viajar al Perú también porque me gustaría reunirme con mi familia peruana.

Práctica 13.2

Let's have a conversation! Create a path as you draw a line from question to answer as you answer the questions. Vary your answers to create different conversations.

Hola. ¿Qué tal?

-Así así. Estoy cansado(a).
-¡Qué lástima! ¿Tienes ganas de descansar?

-Estoy bien gracias.
-Muy bien. ¿Quieres mirar una película esta noche?

-Sí.
-Bueno. Podemos alquilar un video y mirarla en mi casa.

-No.
-Bueno, ¿preferirías cenar juntos?

-Yo preferiría mirar una película en el cine.
-¿Quieres ver algo especial?

- ¡Es una idea fabulosa!
- Bueno, ¿quieres algo especial para comer?

-El problema es que no tengo suficiente dinero.
- No hay problema. Yo te invito entonces.

-No. Pero antes de salir tengo que vestirme.
-No hay problema. Te espero. ¿A qué hora llegarás?

- Yo llegaré a las ocho de la noche a tu casa.
- ¡Uf! Es un poco tarde. ¿Podrías llegar más temprano?

- Mi coche no funciona. ¿Me podrías recoger?
- Tengo que arreglarme. ¿No podrías caminar?

-Creo que no. Es imposible.
- Bueno, entonces, te veo pronto.

- Creo que sí. Trataré de llegar a las seis.
- Bueno. Nos vemos a las seis.

- Bueno. Y, ¿será posible que me lleves a mi casa después?
- Sí, cómo no.

-¿Sabes qué? Después de planear tanto, no tengo energía para salir esta noche.
- Te comprendo. Me siento igual.

- Gracias por invitarme. Nos vemos pronto, ¿verdad?
- Claro que sí, mi amigo(a). Nos vemos.

Práctica 13.3

You need to tell someone how to make a sandwich. Put the following commands in order.

_____ Añada la lechuga y el tomate.

_____ Busque todos los ingredientes en el mercado.

_____ Coma y disfrute el sándwich.

_____ Compre los ingredientes en el supermercado.

_____ Haga una lista de las cosas que necesita.

_____ Lave la lechuga y el tomate.

_____ Lleve todo lo que necesita a la casa.

_____ Ponga el jamón sobre el pan.

_____ Ponga el otro pedazo de pan encima de todo.

_____ Ponga el pan en un plato.

_____ Ponga el queso encima del jamón.

_____ Ponga todos los ingredientes en el carrito.

_____ Ponga todos los ingredientes en el mostrador.

_____ Unte la mayonesa en el pan con el cuchillo. No ponga demasiado.

_____ Unte la mostaza en el pan.

_____ Vaya al supermercado.

Práctica 13.4

Translate the following paragraph to Spanish. Check your work with the answers in the back of the book.

Last week I visited my cousins in San Francisco. I hadn't seen them for many years. My cousin, Eduardo was celebrating his 30th birthday and I wanted to be there to celebrate with him. A month ago my aunt and uncle told me that they would have a party for Eduardo and they begged me to come. But they didn't have to beg. It was a pleasure to go.

During the week in San Francisco, I celebrated the birthday, but I also did many other activities. I spent time with my aunt, uncle and cousins when they took me to the pier and to an elegant restaurant in Chinatown. We went to Alcatraz and they took me in their car across the Golden Gate Bridge. I ate a lot of the delicious bread.

I had a lot of fun with my family during the week in San Francisco, and I would like to visit them again very soon.

Práctica 13.5
Translate the following email to English. Check your work with the answers in the back of the book.

A quien corresponda:

Me gustaría viajar a Puerto Rico, pero necesito ayuda con los preparativos para el viaje. Viajaré con mi esposo y mis dos hijos. Mis hijos tienen ocho y once años. Queremos viajar por un aerolínea comercial y preferiríamos un vuelo directo.

En Puerto Rico necesitaremos una recámara con dos o tres camas. Una de las camas tendrá que ser una cama matrimonial extra grande. La otra cama podrá ser una cama de matrimonio o mejor, dos camas individuales.

Es necesario que el hotel esté cerca de la playa. Esperamos visitar la Fortaleza el Morro, el centro comercial, y varios otros sitios de interés, pero pasaremos la mayoría del tiempo jugando en la playa y tomando el sol. Si Ud. tenga un mapa, por favor muéstremelo porque me gustaría saber dónde están los sitios turísticos en relación del sitio del hotel.

Gracias de antemano,
Sra. O'Gara

Práctica 13.6
Now try translating the following email to Spanish. Check your work with the answers in the back of the book.

To Whom It May Concern:

My wife and I would like to travel to various cities and sites of interest in Peru. We would like for you to help us make preparations for this trip. We will travel in the month of August because it will be winter in Peru and summer in the United States. We have three weeks of vacation during the month of August.

We would like to visit Lima, Cuzco, and Macchu Pichu. Would you be able to recommend some hotels to us? We would like the rooms to have one king-sized bed. We would prefer hotels of three stars or higher. It's very important that the hotels are in the center of the town because we will not rent any car and we are going to have to take busses.

Thank you in advance,
Mr. Salinas

Práctica 13.7
Match the English phrase to the Spanish equivalent.

1. _____ Si yo fuera tú, visitaría el Museo Nacional.

A. I hope that it doesn't rain or that it's too hot either.

2. _____ Yo quisiera que Ud. corte los arbustos.

B. I am glad that you all are here.

3. _____ Me alegro de que Uds. estén aquí.

C. I visited Mexico three years ago.

4. _____ No me gusta que tú no me digas la verdad.

D. She doubts that we will arrive on time.

5. _____ Ojalá que no llueva ni que tampoco haga calor.

E. If I were you, I'd visit the National Museum

6. _____ Por favor, no hable tan rápido.

F. It's important that you read it before signing.

7. _____ Yo visité a México hace tres años.

G. I don't like that you're not telling me the truth.

8. _____ Es importante que tú lo leas antes de firmar.

H. It's obvious that I understand Spanish well.

9. _____ Ella duda que lleguemos a tiempo.

I. I would like you to cut the bushes.

10. _____ Es obvio que yo comprendo bien el español.

J. Please don't speak so quickly.

Práctica 13.8
Translate the following paragraph to English.

Mi hermano viajó a Europa el año pasado. A él le fascina el arte y quería ir a Francia para visitar el Museo Louvre. Mientras viajaba por París, decidió tomar un tren a España. Tenía tiempo y aunque estaba divirtiéndose en Francia, quería ver la arquitectura española de España.

Sabía que los trenes salían a menudo para España. Decidió tomar el tren el lunes por la mañana. Abordó el tren de alta velocidad a las seis de la mañana y llegó en Barcelona a las doce y media de la tarde. ¡El tren viajó a 200 millas por hora! Fue increíble y muy eficiente.

Práctica 13.9
Translate the following letter to English.

Querido Miguel,

¡Saludos de México D.F.! Ojalá que esta carta te encuentre de buena salud.

Hace una semana que estoy aquí en la capital de México y estoy divirtiéndome mucho. Quiero que estés aquí conmigo. Pero yo sé que todavía tienes clases en la universidad. Algún día tendrás que visitar esta ciudad increíble y bonita.

He hecho mucho durante mi primera semana aquí. Primero, unos amigos del programa me recomendaron que me alojara en un hotel cerca del centro comercial. Fue una recomendación excelente porque es un hotel perfecto para mí. Los empleados son muy amables y atentos. Visité el Zócalo, la plaza principal, y el Palacio de Bellas Artes. Tomé un autobús y fui a Teotihuacán. Era un lugar magnífico y muy interesante. Aprendí mucho sobre la historia de México aunque nadie sabe quiénes construyeron esa ciudad original. ¡Saqué un montón de fotos de la pirámide del sol y la pirámide de la luna!

En la semana entrante, visitaré el Museo de Antropología y hablaré con unos estudiantes de la Universidad Autónoma para aprender más de la vida de hoy en la Ciudad de México.

Cuando yo regrese a Miami, tendremos que ir a tomar café. Podré enseñarte mis fotos y hablar de mi experiencia en este país.

Cuídate mucho y escríbeme. Me gustaría recibir noticias de ti. Te extraño mucho.
¡Abrazos y besos a todos!

Con mucho cariño,
Susana

Práctica 13.10
Translate the following letter to Spanish.

Dear Melissa,

Greetings from Glendale, California! I hope that this letter finds you in good health. I have studied Spanish in my class for six weeks, and I am enjoying myself a lot.

Every day I study Spanish. I learn a lot in my classes, but I learn more when I speak with my new friends. I have met some new friends because we speak a lot in our class. We talk about our lives and of the things we like and don't like. I am glad that we can talk and spend time together. They are very nice and friendly.

My teacher asks us to study outside of the classroom. There is a lot to learn! But I already know how to speak Spanish very well!

In the upcoming weeks, I will continue to study and speak Spanish. I hope (may God grant that) I can practice my Spanish with many Spanish speakers. Will you speak with me and help me? I know that you speak Spanish well too. We will have to go have dinner or coffee so that we might practice together.

Write me soon! I miss you a lot! Hugs and kisses to the family!

Love,
Your friend

Appendix
Answers and Translations

Diálogo 1.1

Character A - Good morning, Ma'am.

Character B - Hi. How are you?

Character A - I am very well, thank you. What is your name?

Character B - My name is Alicia González. And you?

Character A - It's nice to meet you, Alicia. My name is Sofía Lorén.

Character B - Sofía Lorén? But you are not the famous model, right?

Character A - Of course not, Alicia. I'm not a model. I am retired now, but I was an accountant. I am also your new neighbor. We bought this house in June. Before, we used to live in Miami.

Character B - Well, it's nice to meet you Sofía. And welcome to the neighborhood.

Questions:

1. *Are the characters in the dialogue men or women?*
   Los personajes son mujeres. *(The characters are women.)*
2. *Where are they? In a street near Sofía's house or in a supermarket?*
   Están en la calle cerca de la casa de Sofía. *(They are in the street near Sofía's house.)*
3. *What time is it? Is it 2:00pm or 10:00am?*
   Son las diez de la mañana. *(It's 10:00am…"Buenos días tells us it's morning!)*
4. *What is Sofía's profession now?*
   Ella está jubilada. *(She is retired.)*
5. *Where did Sofía live before buying the new house in June?*
   Ella vivía en Miami. *(She used to live in Miami.)*

Diálogo 1.2

Tomás –	Hi, friend. How's everything going?
Francsico -	Okay, thanks. And you?
Tomás –	I'm well. My name is Thomas. And you? What's your name?
Francisco –	My name is Francisco. I've been studying Spanish for six weeks and I don't understand a lot.
Tomás –	It's a pleasure, Francisco. You speak Spanish very well! Where are you from?
Francisco –	I'm from Europe – from Germany. And you?
Tomás -	I'm from Columbia – from Bogotá. But now I live here in Glendale, California.
	I like California a lot. It's always good weather and the beaches are very pretty.
Francisco -	I agree. Well, Francisco, what do you like to do in your free time? Do you have some favorite hobbies/pastimes?
Tomás –	Let's see… I like to travel a lot. I also like to read mystery novels and to spend time with my family and friends.
Francisco –	I love to spend time with my family. I like to listen to music and watch movies in the movie theater.
Tomás -	Do you like sports?
Francisco –	No, I don't like sports. But I like art. And, do you like art also?
Tomás -	Yes, more or less… not much. My best friend loves art.
Francisco –	Well, Thomas. It was a pleasure. I have to go to my house. See you soon.
Tomás –	Until next time.

Questions

1. *How long has Francisco been studying Spanish?*
   Hace seis meses que estudia español. *(He's been studying Spanish for 6 weeks.)*

2. *Does Francisco understand a lot or a little Spanish?*
   Comprende poco español. *(He understands a little Spanish.)*

3. *Where is Thomas from?*
   Es de Colombia – de Bogotá. *(He's from Columbia – from Bogota.)*

4. *Where do Thomas and Francisco live now?*

Ellos viven en California. *(They live in California.)*

5. *What does Francisco like to do in his free time?*

A Francisco le gusta pasar tiempo con su familia, escuchar música y mirar películas en el cine. *(He likes to spend time with his family, listen to music and watch movies in the movie theater.)*

6. *What do Thomas and Francisco like to do?*

Les gusta pasar tiempo con familia. *(They like to spend time with family.)*

7. *Do Thomas and Francisco like sports?*

No, a Tomás le gustan los deportes, pero a Francisco no le gustan los deportes. *(No. Thomas likes sports, but Francisco doesn't like sports.)*

8. *Who likes to read novels?*

A Tomás le gusta leer novelas. *(Thomas likes to read novels.)*

9. *Who doesn't like art much?*

A Tomás no le gusta mucho el arte. *(Thomas doesn't like art much.)*

10. *Where is Francisco going?*

Francisco va a su casa. *(Francisco is going to his house.)*

Práctica 1.1

Answers will vary.

Translation of Questions:
1. What is your partner's name?
2. Where is he/she from?
3. What does your partner like to do in his/her free time?
4. Does your partner like or not like the same activities as you?
5. Who has to go? You or your partner? Where do you have to go?

Práctica 1.2

1. *Where are the people in this picture? Are they in the house, the libarary, or in the classroom?*
   Están en la clase. = *They are in the classroom.*

2. *Who is the woman with the glasses? Is she a saleswoman, a principal, a teacher or a librarian?*
   Ella es maestra. = *She is a teacher.*

3. *What are the people talking about? Are they talking about a composition, an exam, or about all the grades in a class?*
   Hablan de todas las notas en una clase. = *They are talking about all the grades in a class.*

4. *Does the boy have good or bad grades?*
   Tiene buenas notas. = *He has good grades.*

5. *What sport does the boy like most? Does he like soccer or baseball?*
   Al chico le gusta más el fútbol. = *He likes soccer more.*

6. *Is the boy worried or calm/tranquil?*
   El chico está tranquilo. = *The boy is calm/tranquil.*

7. *Is the boy's mom happy or worried?*
   Ella está contenta. = *She is happy.*

8. *What is the teacher doing... explaining the grades or talking about goals from the soccer game?*
   La maestra explica las notas. = *The teacher is explaining the grades.*

Práctica 2.1

1. bailan	9. aprendo
2. vendo	10. creen
3. sube	11. comemos
4. esperas	12. vives
5. leemos	13. trabaja
6. recibís	14. cantas
7. viajamos	15. reciben
8. llegan	16. necesito

Práctica 2.2

1. *Where are the people? Are they in the airport or in the hotel?*
Están en el hotel. = *They are in the hotel.*

2. *What is the woman in the armchair doing? Do you believe she is waiting for another person or is she resting?*
La mujer en el sillón lee. Creo que ella descansa (or) espera a otra persona. = *The woman in the archair is reading. I believe that she is resting (or) waiting for another person.*

3. *Does the woman at the counter need the bill or a room? What is in the envelope?*
Necesita la cuenta. La cuenta está en el sobre. = *She needs the bill. The bill is in the envelope.*

4. *Is the man with the suitcase mad because he is waiting in the line or because he needs help with his suitcase?*
Está enojado porque espera en la cola. = *He is mad because he is waiting in the line.*

5. *Is the man with the suitcase arriving or leaving?*
El hombre con la maleta llega / sale. = *The man with the suitcase is arriving / leaving.*

6. *Does the man with the suitcase need a room?*
Answers will vary.

7. *Who is the tall man with the hat? Is he a customer or employee of the hotel?*
El hombre alto con el sombrero es empleado del hotel. = *The tall man with the hat is an employee of the hotel.*

8. *What is man with the suitcase looking at? Is he looking at his watch or his telephone?*
El hombre con la maleta mira su reloj. = *The man with the suitcase is looking at his watch.*

9. *Is it a modern or traditional hotel?*
Es un hotel moderno. = *It's a modern hotel.*

10. *Does this scene occur in the hotel room or in the hotel lobby?*

Esta escena ocurre en el vestíbulo del hotel. = *This scene occurs in the hotel lobby.*

Práctica 2.3

These would be the questions you would ask your partner. The answers will vary.

1. ¿Sales mucho con tus amigos los fines de semana?

   Do you go out with your friends on weekends?

2. ¿Conoces bien a una persona famosa?

   Do you know a famous person well?

3. ¿Reconoces fácilmente a las personas?

   Do you recognize people easily?

4. ¿Sabes tocar un instrumento?

   Do you know how to play an instrument?

5. ¿Haces ejercicio todos los días?

   Do you do exercise every day?

6. ¿Les das regalos a tus amigos de vez en cuando?

   Do you give gifts to your friends once in a while?

7. ¿Pones tus llaves en el mismo lugar cada vez que entras en tu casa?

   Do you put your keys in the same place every time you enter your house?

8. ¿Traes comida o bebidas a las fiestas?

   Do you bring food or drinks to parties?

Práctica 2.4

1. Mi mamá **hierve** el agua para hacer té.

   My mom boils the water to make tea.

2. Uds. **prefieren** ir al restaurante chino, ¿no?

   You all prefer to go to the Chinese restaurant, right?

3. ¿Quiénes **se despiertan** temprano por las mañanas?

   Who all wakes up early in the mornings?

4. Yo no **entiendo** la pregunta.

   I don't understand the question.

5. Mi familia **quiere** pasar dos semanas en España.

   My family wants to spend two weeks in Spain.

6. Yo no **pierdo** muchas cosas.

   I don't lose many things.

7. **Nieva** mucho en las montañas.

   It snows a lot in the mountains.

156

8. El policía siempre **defiende** a la gente.
   The police officer defends the people.

Práctica 2.5

1. *What is the woman thinking about? Is she thinking about watching a movie or taking a cruise?*

   Piensa en tomar un crucero. *(She's thinking about taking a cruise.)*

2. *Does the man prefer to take a cruise or to watch television at home?*

   El hombre prefiere mirar la televisión en casa. *(The man prefers to watch television at home.)*

3. *Is the date starting or ending? How do you know?*

   La cita empieza. No hay comida en la mesa, pero los platos están. La botella de vino está en la mesa. *(The date is starting. There's no food on the table, but the plates are there. The bottle of wine is on the table.)*

4. *Are the people having a snack or eating dinner?*

   Las personas cenan. *(The people are eating dinner.)*

5. *Are the two having fun? How do you know?*

   Sí, se divierten porque sonríen. *(Yes, they're having fun because they are smiling.)*

Práctica 2.6

1. Do you go to bed before or after 11:00PM?

   Me acuesto antes de las 11:00PM. (I go to bed before 11:00PM)
   Me acuesto después de las 11:00PM. (I go to bed after 11:00PM)

2. Generally, do you eat lunch at home or in a restaurant?

   Generalmente almuerzo en casa. (Generally, I eat lunch at home.)
   Generalmente almuerzo en un restaurante. (Generally, I eat lunch in a restaurant.)

3. Do you tell good jokes?

   Sí, yo cuento chistes buenos. (Yes, I tell good jokes.)
   (or) No, yo no cuento chistes buenos. (No, I don't tell good jokes.)

4. Do you remember names or faces of people better?

      Yo recuerdo mejor los nombres de las personas. (I remember people's names better.)

      Yo recuerdo mejor las caras de las personas. (I remember people's faces better.)

5. Can you do something interesting? What is it?

      Yo puedo…(infinitive)

      I can …

      Ejemplo: Yo puedo patinar. = I can skate.

Práctica 2.7

1. ¿Compites en unos deportes?

    Sí, yo compito en … (Yes, I compete in …)

    or

    No, yo no compito en ningún deporte. (No, I don't compete in any sport.)

2. ¿Qué sabor pides en una heladería?

    Pido el (vainilla, fresa, chocolate) en una heladería. (I order (vanilla, strawberry, chocolate) in an ice cream shop.)

3. De qué te ríes?

    Me río de… (I laugh at…)

4. ¿Quién sirve las comidas en tu casa?

    (Answers will vary)

5. ¿Sigues las reglas?

      Sí, yo sigo las reglas. (or) No, no sigo las reglas. (Yes, I follow the rules. / No, I don't follow the rules.)

6. ¿Mides dos veces y cortas una vez?

      Sí, yo mido dos veces y corto una vez. (Yes, I measure twice and cut once.)

Práctica 2.8

1. Is the narrator with Carolina at this moment?

      No, el narrador no está con Carolina en este momento.

      No, the narrator isn't with Carolina at this moment.

2. What is Carolina's profession?

> Ahora Carolina es dueña de una tienda de ropa atlética.
>
> Now Carolina is an owner of an athletic clothing store.

3. What kind of clothing does Carolina sell in her store?

> Carolina vende ropa atlética en su tienda.
>
> Carolina sells athletic clothing in her store.

4. What does the narrator hear about Carolina's cousin?

> La prima viene con Carolina para visitar a los Estados Unidos.
>
> The cousin is coming with Carolina to visit the US.

5. When are Victoria and Carolina going to arrive the US?

> Van a llegar a los Estados Unidos en dos semanas.
>
> They are going to arrive in two weeks.

Práctica 2.9

1. What are you afraid of?
   Tengo miedo de… (I'm afraid of…)

2. Do you believe that some people are lucky and others aren't? Why?
   Sí, creo que unas personas tienen suerte y otras no porque …(Yes, I believe that some people are lucky and others aren't because…)
   No, no creo que unas personas tienen suerte y otras no porque…(No, I don't believe that some people are lucky and others aren't because…)

3. Do you feel sleepy every day? How often do you feel sleepy?
   Sí, tengo sueño todos los días. (Yes, I feel sleepy every day.)
   No, no tengo sueño todos los días. (No, I don't feel sleepy every day.)
   Tengo sueño… (I feel sleepy…)

4. Are you generally hungry in the mornings?
   Sí, generalmente tengo hambre por las mañanas. (Yes, I'm generally hungry in the mornings.)
   No, generalmente no tengo hambre por las mañanas. (No, I don't generally feel hungry in the mornings.)

5. How old should a person be to drink alcochol?
   Para beber alcohol, una persona debe tener_____ años. (To drink alcohol, a person should be ____ years old.)

6. How old should a person be to get married?
   Una persona debe tener ____ años para casarse. (A person should be ____ years old to get married.)

7. How do you know that a person is successful? When does a person have success? Are you successful? Why?
   Sé que una persona tiene éxito cuando... (I know a person is successful when...)
   Sí, yo tengo éxito porque.... (Yes, I'm successful because...)
   No, no tengo éxito porque... (No I'm not successful because...)

8. After eating ice cream are you thirsty?
   Sí, después de comer helado, tengo sed. (Yes, after eating ice cream I am thirsty.)
   No, después de comer helado, no tengo sed. (No, after eating ice cream, I am not thirsty.)

Práctica 2.10
1. Who is thirsty?
   Patricia tiene sed. (Patricia is thirsty.)

2. Who feelis like swimming?
   Tomás tiene ganas de nadar. (Thomas feels like swimming.)

3. Who is successful?
   Dorotea tiene éxito. (Dorothy is successful.)

4. Who feels embarrassed/ashamed?
   Carlitos tiene vergüenza. (Carlitos feels embarrassed/ashamed.)

5. Who is hungry?
   Miguel tiene hambre. (Michael is hungry.)

6. Who is very lucky?
   Juan tiene mucha suerte. (Juan is very lucky.)

7. Who has to make the bed?
   Emilio tiene que hacer la cama. (Emilio has to make the bed.)

8. Who is cold?

> Susana tiene frío. (Susana is cold.)

Práctica 3.1

1. P   (rule # 1)   6. P   (rule # 2)

2. I   (rule # 2)   7. I   (rule # 4) and (rule # 5)

3. P   (rule # 3)   8. P   (rule # 2)

4. I   (rule # 5)   9. I   (rule # 4) and (rule # 5)

5. P   (rule # 1)   10. P (rule # 1)

Diálogo 3.1

Tomás: Alisa, what **were** you like when you **were** eight years old? **Were** you obedient or disobedient?

Alisa: I **was** very obedient. I always **used to listen** to my parents and I **would follow** all the rules.

Tomás: I don't doubt it. You are still an angel.

Alisa: Oy, Tomás... you are very nice. And you? What **were** you like when you **were** a little boy?

Tomás: You don't want to know. I **was** very disobedient. I always **used to fight** with my siblings. And I never **would help** at home. I **was** very lazy. But I always **would get** good grades in school because I **was** very intelligent and diligent with my homework.

Alisa: What more? What **would you do** with your friends? **Did you have** a lot of friends?

Tomás: Yes, yes. I **had** friends, but not many. Only the children that **lived** near my house. We **used to ride** our bikes or **would play** video games. Sometimes we **would go** to the park to play basketball. We really **liked** to spend time outside, playing sports.

Práctica 3.2

1. What was Alisa like when she was little? Obedient or disobedient? And Thomas?

   Alisa era obediente y Tomás era desobediente.

   Alisa was obedient and Thomas was disobedient.

2. Is Alisa different or the same from when she was a little girl?

   Alisa era la misma.

   Alisa was the same.

3. Why does Thomas say that he was lazy?

   Tomás dice que era perezoso porque no ayudaba en casa.

   Thomas says that he was lazy because he would never help at home.

4. Where would Thomas and his friends go to play sports?

   Tomás y sus amigos iban al parque para jugar a los deportes.

   Thomas and his friends used to go to the park to play sports.

Práctica 3.3

1. When you were little, were you obedient or disobedient?

   Cuando era niño(a), yo era obediente/desobediente?

   When I was little, I was…

2. When you were little, did you play an instrument?

   Cuando era niño(a), yo tocaba…

   When I was little I played…

   Cuando era niño(a), no tocaba ningún instrumento.

   When I was little, I didn't play any instrument.

3. Where did you live?

   Yo vivía en…

   I lived in …

4. When you were little, did you practice a sport? Which sport?

   Cuando era niño(a), practicaba …

   When I was little, I practiced…

   Cuando era niño(a), no practicaba ningún deporte.

   When I was little, I didn't practice any sport.

5. Did you used to go on vacation during summers?

 Sí, yo iba de vacaciones los veranos.

 Yes, I went on vacations during the summers.

 No, no iba de vacaciones los veranos.

 No I didn't go on vacations during the summers.

Práctica 3.4

 My grandmother was a very special person for me. **My grandmother's** name was **Clara**, and **she** was very **nice** and **caring**. She always would **smile** when I visited **her**. She **lived** in **Glendale, California**, very **near** my family's house.   She was from **Germany** originally. **My grandmother** used to **take care of the neighborhood kids**. She earned a living that way. **She** spent a lot of time **in the house**. **She would clean** a lot and **her house was always perfect**. **She cooked** well, and liked to **play games with the kids**. She also liked to **listen to piano music**. She liked **animals** and she had a pet. She had **a bird that was always in his cage in the kitchen of her house**. **The bird's** name was **Timmy**. Many times **my grandmother and I bathed Timmy**. **My grandmother** loved **her husband, my grandfather** a lot. But my grandfather **died when they were both 59 years old**. **My grandmother lived along after the death of my grandfather**.   **But** she always was **happy** because she was an **optimist**, and in that way she lived a very **happy** life.

Práctica 3.5
1. I traveled to Spain.
 ¿<u>Viajaste</u> a España? (Did you travel to Spain?)

2. I ate an exotic meal once.
 ¿<u>Comiste</u> una comida exótica una vez? (Did you eat an exotic meal once?)

3. I lived in another country for more than one year.
 ¿<u>Viviste</u> en otro país por más de un año? (Did you live in another country for more than one year?

 one year?

4. I wrote an autobiography.
 ¿<u>Escribiste</u> una autobiografía? (Did you write an autobiography?)

5. I sold something that I didn't want to sell.
 ¿<u>Vendiste</u> algo que no querías vender? (Did you sell something that you didn't want to sell?

 sell?

6. I watched a movie last night.
   ¿<u>Miraste</u> una película anoche? (Did you watch a movie last night?)

7. I lost and found an important thing recently.
   ¿<u>Perdiste</u> y <u>encontraste</u> una cosa importante recientemente?

8. I worked until very late last night.
   ¿<u>Trabajaste</u> hasta muy tarde anoche?

9. I slept for less than seven hours last night.
   ¿<u>Dormiste</u> por menos de siete horas anoche?

10. I sang in the shower this morning.
    ¿<u>Cantaste</u> en la ducha esta mañana?

11. I read many books last year.
    ¿<u>Leíste</u> muchos libros el año pasado?

12. I studied Spanish last night.
    ¿<u>Estudiaste</u> el español anoche?

13. I bought something very expensive and unnecessary once.
    ¿<u>Compraste</u> algo muy caro e innecesario una vez?

14. I participated in a sport in high school.
    ¿<u>Participaste</u> en un deporte en la escuela secundaria?

15. I drank coffee this morning.
    ¿<u>Tomaste</u> café esta mañana?

16. I listened to good music in a concert recently.
    ¿<u>Escuchaste</u> música buena en un concierto recientemente?

17. I cleaned my house this past weekend.
    ¿<u>Limpiaste</u> tu casa este fin de semana pasado?

18. I went to bed late last night.
    ¿<u>Te acostaste</u> tarde anoche?

19. I met my best friend in a class in elementary school.
    ¿<u>Conociste</u> a tu mejor amigo(a) en una clase en la escuela primaria?

20. I read an entire book more than two times.
    ¿<u>Leíste</u> un libro entero más de dos veces?

21. I lived in a place for more than ten years.
    ¿<u>Viviste</u> en un lugar por más de diez años?

22. I received a ticket this year.
    ¿<u>Recibiste</u> una multa este año?

23. I received good grades in high school.
    ¿<u>Recibiste</u> buenas notas en la escuela secundaria?

24. I got up early this morning.
    ¿<u>Te levantaste</u> temprano esta mañana?

25. I moved many times during my youth.
    ¿<u>Te mudaste</u> muchas veces durante tu juventud?

Práctica 3.6

1. Yo **toqué** la guitarra anoche. (I played the guitar last night.)
2. Yo le **entregué** la tarea a la maestra. (I delivered/turned in the homework to the teacher.)
3. ¿Les **explicó** la maestra la lección a los estudiantes hoy? (Did the teacher explain the lesson to the students today?)
4. Yo **jugué** al tenis ayer por la tarde. (I played tennis yesterday in the afternoon.)
5. **Llegaste** tú tarde a la clase anoche? (Did you arrive late to class last night?)
6. Yo **saqué** mi pluma de mi mochila al llegar a la clase. (I took out my pen from my backpack upon arriving to the class.)
7. Mi esposo y yo **pagamos** la cuenta y salimos del restaurante. (My husband and I paid the bill and we left the restaurant.)
8. ¿**Cruzaron** Uds. la calle para llegar al cine? (Did you all cross the street to arrive to the movie theater?)
9. El programa **empezó/comenzó** a las ocho de la noche. (The program began at 8:00PM.)
10. Mi información no es correcta. Yo **me equivoqué**. (My information isn't correct. I made a mistake.)

Práctica 3.7

1. Mis hijos durmieron por unas horas anoche.

2. ¿Se despidieron tus amigos de ti?

3. Me reí cuando oí el chiste.

4. Sr. y Sra. Molina, ¿prefirieron (Uds.) el libro o la película?

5. Sintió su decisión?

6. Ellos no mintieron; ellos se divirtieron mucho.

7. ¿Qué pidieron Uds.?

8. El maestro (La maestra) repitió las palabras nuevas.

Práctica 3.8

1. Él creyó la historia.
2. ¿Oyeron Uds. las noticias?
3. ¿Quién se cayó?
4. ¿Leyó él el artículo hoy?

Práctica 3.9

1. ¿Trajiste una pluma a clase esta noche?

   Sí, traje una pluma a clase esta noche. (Yes, I brought a pen to class tonight.)

   No, no traje ninguna pluma a clase esta noche. (No, I didn't bring a pen to class tonight.)

2. ¿Condujiste a un lugar interesante hoy?

   Sí, conduje a un lugar interesante hoy.(Yes, I drove to an interesting place today.)

   No, no conduje a ningún lugar interesante hoy.(No, I didn't drive to any place interesting today.)

3. ¿Qué hiciste para la cena esta noche?

   Yo hice... para la cena esta noche. (I made... for dinner tonight.)

4. ¿Pudiste dormir bien anoche?

   Sí, pude dormir bien anoche. (Yes, I was able to sleep well last night.)

   No, no pude dormir bien anoche. (No, I wasn't able to sleep well last night.)

5. ¿Dónde estuviste ayer?

   Yo estuve en... ayer. (I was in ... yesterday.)

6. ¿Cómo supiste de esta clase?

   Supe de esta clase ... del internet, de un amigo, de un anuncio, del folleto etc. (I found out about this class from... the internet, a friend, an advertisement, the brochure etc.)

Práctica 3.10

My friend, Katarina, went to Orlando for her work. (1. Where did Katarina go? To Miami or to Orlando?) **She had to get together with a group of colleagues there.** (2. Did she have to get together with family, with friends, or with people from her work?) **But also she had time to enjoy herself a little.** (3. Did she have time only for work? Or did she have time to relax?) **And so it was that she decided to visit the Magic Kingdom of Disney on Friday, a day before leaving.** (4. Where did Katarina decide to go to have fun? Did she decide to go to the town center or to an amusement park?) (5. On what day did she visit the park?) **She couldn't drive there. She managed to take a tram that took people from the hotel to the park.** (6. Did Katarina go to the park in her car? How did Katarina arrive to the park?) **She walked a lot that day because she was looking for her favorite roller coaster – the "Matterhorn".** (7. Why did Katarina walk a lot? Was she looking for a restaurant or a specific attraction?) **She managed to ride on many attractions, but she didn't see the "Matterhorn".** (8. Did Katarina ride on other attractions or did she only ride the "Matterhorn"?) **Finally she asked for help from a very nice employee of the park. His name was Christopher, and from him, Katarina found out the answer why she couldn't find the "Matterhorn".** (9. From whom did Katarina ask help? From an employee of the Magic Kingdom or from a friend?) **The employee told Katarina that the "Matterhorn" wasn't in the Magic Kingdom. He told her that the "Matterhorn" was only in Disneyland.** (10. What did Katarina find out? Did she find out that the "Matterhorn" was in another part of the park or that the ride wasn't in the park?) **Katarina was a little sad after hearing that her favorite ride wasn't in the park.** (11. Was Katarina mad or sad? Why was she sad?) **But she still had fun on the other rides. Although there were a lot of people in long lines, Katarina rode on a lot of roller coasters and saw some funny and beautiful shows.** (12. Were the lines for the rides short or long? Did Katarina enjoy herself or no?) **At 10:00, she watched fireworks and listened to the music. Afterwards, she left.** (13. Did Katarina have time or not to watch the fireworks show?) **She didn't want to spend much money and so she didn't go into the stores and she didn't bring one souvenir. She only brought the memory of a happy day in the Magic Kingdom.** (14. Did Katarina buy or not buy some souvenirs? Why didn't she buy souvenirs from the store?)

1. fue a Orlando
2. con colegas
3. tuvo tiempo para relajarse
4. decidió ir a un parque de diversiones
5. fue el viernes
6. No fue al parque en su coche; fue en tranvía
7. buscaba una atracción específica
8. Katarina anduvo en otras atracciones
9. le pidió ayuda de un empleado
10. Supo que el "Matterhorn" no estaba en el parque

11. Estuvo triste porque su atracción favorita no estaba en el parque.
12. Las líneas fueron largas. Sí, se divirtió
13. Sí tuvo tiempo para mirar el espectáculo de fuegos artificiales
14. No compró recuerdos porque no quería gastar dinero

Práctica 3.11
Answers will vary

Práctica 3.12
Answers will vary

Práctica 3.13
Cuando yo (fui, **era**) niña, yo (viví, **vivía**) en una casa pequeña en los suburbios. Mi papá me (llevó, **llevaba**) a la escuela cada mañana. Mi escuela (estuvo, **estaba**) cerca de mi casa pero a mí no me (gustó, **gustaba**) caminar sola. Pero un día, yo (**decidí**, decidía) caminar con mi vecina a la escuela. Ella (se llamó, **se llamaba**) Rosita y ella (vivió, **vivía**) en la casa enfrente de la mía.

En ese día, (hizo, **hacía**) mucho frío por la mañana. Yo (**me puse**, me ponía) la chaqueta y las botas negras antes de salir de la casa. Yo (**fui**, iba) a la casa de Rosita y (**toqué**, tocaba) a la puerta. Ella (**abrió**, abría) la puerta inmediatamente y (**se sonrió**, se sonreía). Su mamá (**se despidió** , se despedía) de nosotras y ella (**cerró**, cerraba) la puerta. Rosita y yo (**caminamos**, caminábamos) por una cuadra. Entonces, nosotras (**vimos**, veíamos) a nuestra amiga, Ana, y a su hermano, José. Ana y su hermano siempre (caminan, **caminaban**) juntos a la escuela. Todos nosotros (**empezamos**, empezábamos) a caminar juntos. Entonces, (**empezó**, empezaba) a llover. (**Nos reímos**, Nos reíamos) y (**corrimos**, corríamos) tan rápido como posible hacia la escuela.

En ese momento, mi papá (**llegó**, llegaba) en su carro. Nosotros (**subimos**, subíamos) en su carro y él nos (**llevó**, llevaba) a la escuela.

Práctica 3.14
Cuando yo (tuve, **tenía**) dieciséis años, yo (**fui**, iba) al Perú para vivir con una familia peruana. Yo (**viajé**, viajaba) con un programa de intercambio. Antes de salir, yo (tuve, **tenía**) mucho miedo. Yo no (supe, **sabía**) qué esperar. Yo no (supe, **sabía**) mucho de la vida en Perú ni de la cultura de la gente.

El día que yo (**salí**, salía) yo me (**despedí**, despedía) de mi familia y yo (**viajé**, viajaba) por avión hacia Miami. En Miami, nosotros (**aprendimos**, aprendíamos) de unas costumbres en Perú. Por ejemplo, nosotros (**aprendimos**, aprendíamos) que las personas se besan cuando se saludan. Nosotros (**aprendimos**, aprendíamos) que la gente come la comida principal cada día a las dos de la tarde durante las horas de la siesta.

Después de dos días en Miami, nosotros (**viajamos**, viajábamos) al Perú donde yo (**conocí**, conocía) a mi familia. Durante los siguientes meses, yo (**asistí**, asistía) a la escuela, (**conocí**, conocía) a muchos nuevos amigos, y (**descubrí**, descubría) que los peruanos (fueron, **eran**) muy simpáticos y amables. Una semana, yo (**fui**, iba) a Machu Picchu y (**vi**, veía) las ruinas de la ciudad antigua encima de las montañas de los Andes. (Fue, **Era**) muy bonita e interesante.

Yo (**viví**, vivía) en Perú por solo tres meses, pero yo (**aprendí**, aprendía) mucho. El viaje (**cambió**, cambiaba) mi vida para siempre.

Práctica 3.15

1. fuimos
2. queríamos
3. Era
4. era
5. Había
6. esperábamos
7. llegó
8. llevaba
9. era
10. eran
11. empezaron
12. pudimos
13. empezaron
14. taconeó
15. giró
16. hicieron
17. escuchamos
18. miramos
19. era
20. divertimos

Práctica 3.16

1. How many people were working when the thief arrived at the counter?
   Tres personas trabajaban cuando el ladrón llegó al mostrador.
   Three people were working when the thief arrived to the counter.

2. What did the three tellers do when the thief took out the gun?
   El cajero levantó las manos; una de las cajeras le llamó a la policía. La otra se escondió detrás del mostrador.
   The (male) teller raised his hands; one of the (female) tellers called the police. The other hid behind the counter.

3. How do you know that the tellers were afraid of the man?
   Porque el hombre levantó las manos y la mujer le llamó a la policía. Las bocas están abiertas y se ven asustados.
   Because the man raised his hands and the woman called the police. Their mouths are open and they look scared.

4. Do you think the coins and bills were already on the counter before the thief arrived?
   Or do you think they put the money on the counter because the thief ordered them to
   do it?
   Creo que pusieron el dinero en el mostrador porque les ordenó hacerlo.
   I think they put the money on the counter because the thief ordered them to do it.

5. Why was the thief wearing a mask? Why did he wear a cap?
   Llevaba la máscara para esconder su cara. Llevaba una gorra como parte de su disfraz.
   He was wearing a mask to hide his face. He was wearing a cap as part of his disguise.

6. Who did the teller call? With whom did she speak? Do you think she made the call
   when the thief appeared or that she was already talking when he entered the bank?
   Answers will vary.

Diálogo 4.1
Teacher:	Diego, Do you have your pen, paper and book?
Diego:	Yes, Ma'am, I have my pen, paper, and book in my backpack.
Teacher:	And where did you put your backpack?
Diego:	I put my backpack in the classroom.

Diálogo 4.2
Teacher:	Diego, do you have your pen, paper, and book?
Diego:	Yes, Ma'am, I have them in my backpack.
Teacher:	And where did you put your backpack?
Diego:	I put it in the classroom.

Diálogo 4.3
Miguel:	Ana, are you going to leave the tip for the waiter?
Ana:	Yes, Miguel. I already left the tip for the waiter.
Miguel:	Well, then, do you want to go to see the movie now? I have the schedule for the movie theater here. Do you want to see the movie schedule?
Ana:	Yes, I want to see the movie schedule.

Diálogo 4.4
Miguel:	Ana, are you going to leave the tip for the waiter?
Ana:	Yes, Miguel. I already left it for him.
Miguel:	Well, then do you want to see the movie now? I have the schedule for the movie theater here. Do you want to see it?
Ana:	Yes, I want to see it.

Práctica 4.1

1. Suzy cooks Bob a cake.
    1. Subject = **Suzy**
    2. Verb = **Cooks**
    3. **Suzy cooks**... who?/what? = **a cake**

2. We are watching the old movies in the living room.
    1. Subject = **We**
    2. Verb = **are watching**
    3. **We are watching**... who?/what? = **the old movies**

3. Juana saw Carlos and me yesterday in the store.
    1. Subject = **Juana**
    2. Verb = **saw**
    3. **Juana saw** who?/what? = **Carlos and me**

4. I invited Tomás and Julia to the party.
    1. Subject = **I**
    2. Verb = **invited**
    3. **I invited** ...who?/what? = **Tomás and Julia**

Práctica 4.2

1. Suzy cooks Bob *a cake*.
    Suzy cooks **it** for him.

2. We are watching *the old movies* in the living room.
    We are watching **them** in the living room.

3. Juana saw *Carlos and me* yesterday in the store.
    Juana saw **us** yesterday in the store.

4. I invited *Tomás and Julia* to the party.
    I invited **them** to the party.

Práctica 4.3

1. Katia tomó la aspirina.
   1. Sujeto/Subject = **Katia**
   2. Verbo/Verb = **tomó**
   3. **Katia tomó**... ¿Quién? / ¿Qué? (who?/what?) = **la aspirina**
   (direct object noun) **la aspirina** = (D.O. Pronoun) **la**

2. Yo vi a Alicia y a Verónica en la escuela ayer.
   1. Sujeto/Subject = **Yo**
   2. Verbo/Verb = **vi**
   3. **Yo vi** ... ¿ Quién? / ¿Qué?   (who?/what?) = **a Alicia y a Verónica**
   (direct object noun) **a Alicia y a Verónica** = (D.O. Pronoun) **las**

3. Mis amigos comprenden a mí muy bien.
   1. Sujeto/Subject = **Mis amigos**
   2. Verbo/Verb = **comprenden**
   3. **Mis amigos comprenden** ... Quién? / ¿Qué?   (who?/what?) = **a mí**
   (direct object noun) **a mí** = (D.O. Pronoun)   **me**

4. Uds. invitaron a mi hermano y a mí a cenar en el restaurante, ¿no?
   1. Sujeto/Subject = **Uds.**
   2. Verbo/Verb = **invitaron**
   3. **Uds. invitaron** ... Quién? / ¿Qué?   (who?/what?) = **a mi hermano y a mí**
   (direct object noun) **a mi hermano y a mí** = (D.O. Pronoun)   **nos**

Práctica 4.4

1. Katia la tomó. = *Katia took it.*
2. Yo las vi en la escuela ayer. = *I saw them in the school yesterday.*
3. Mis amigos me comprenden muy bien. = *My friends understand me very well.*
4. Uds. nos invitaron a cenar en el restaurante, ¿no? = *You all invited us to eat dinner in the restaurant, right?*

Práctica 4.5

1. Ella la vendió ayer.
2. (Nosotros) los recibimos anoche.
3. Manuel, ¿la ves?
4. Te invité a mi fiesta, Diego.
5. ¿Quién la escribió?

6. ¿Me comprende (entiende), Señor?
7. (Yo) los voy a leer. (or) (Yo) voy a leerlos.
8. Te amo (quiero).
9. ¿Quién te dijo, Susana?
10. (Nosotros) os/los vamos a visitar en el verano. (or) (Nosotros) vamos a vistarlos (visitaros) en el verano.

Práctica 4.6

1. ¿Viste <u>a tus amigos</u> hoy? = *Did you see your friends today?*
   ¿Los viste hoy? = *Did you see them today?*
   Sí, los vi hoy. = *Yes, I saw them today.* (or) No, no los vi hoy. = *No, I didn't see them today.*

2. ¿Bebiste <u>(el) café</u> esta mañana? = *Did you drink coffee this morning?*
   ¿Lo bebiste esta mañana? = *Did you drink it this morning?*
   Sí, lo bebí esta mañana. = *Yes, I drank it this morning.* (or) No, no lo bebí esta mañana. = *No, I didn't drink it today.*

3. ¿Explicó la maestra <u>la lección</u>? = *Did the teacher explain the lesson?*
   ¿La explicó la maestra? = *Did the teacher explain it?*
   Sí, la maestra la explicó. = *Yes, the teacher explained it.* (or) No, la maestra no la explicó. = *No, the teacher didn't explain it.*

4. ¿Dónde pusiste <u>tu libro de español</u>? = *Where did you put your Spanish book?*
   ¿Dónde lo pusiste? = *Where did you put it?*
   Lo puse en… = *I put it in…*

5. ¿Comprendes tú <u>los pronombres directos</u>? = *Do you understand the direct object pronouns?*
   ¿Los comprendes tú? = *Do you understand them?*
   Sí, (yo) los comprendo. = *Yes, I understand them.* (or) No, no los comprendo. = *No, I don't understand them.*

6. ¿Vas a estudiar <u>el español</u> esta noche? = *Are you going to study Spanish tonight?*
   ¿Lo vas a estudiar esta noche? (or) ¿Vas a estudiarlo esta noche? = *Are you going to study it tonight?*
   Sí, (yo) lo voy a estudiar esta noche. (or) Sí, (yo) voy a estudiarlo esta noche. = *Yes, I'm going to study it tonight.* (or) No, (yo) no lo voy a estudiar esta noche. (or) No, (yo) no voy a estudiarlo esta noche. = *No, I'm not going to study it tonight.*

Práctica 4.7

1. Suzy cooks Bob a cake.
   1. Subject = **Suzy**
   2. Verb = **cooks**
   3. **Suzy cooks**... who?/what? = **a cake**
   4. **Suzy cooks a cake**... to whom?/ for whom? = **for Bob** = Indirect Object Noun

2. We left the tip for the waiter.
   1. Subject = **We**
   2. Verb = **left**
   3. **We left** ... who?/what? = **the tip**
   4. **We left the tip**... to whom?/ for whom? = **for the waiter** = Indirect Object Noun

3. I told you the truth.
   1. Subject = **I**
   2. Verb = **told**
   3. **I told**... who?/what? = **the truth**
   4. **I told the truth** ... to whom?/ for whom? = **you** = Indirect Object Noun

4. She gave me the money.
   1. Subject = **She**
   2. Verb = **gave**
   3. **She gave**... who?/what? = **the money**
   4. **She gave the money**... to whom?/ for whom? = **me** = Indirect Object Noun

5. I am going to write you a letter.
   1. Subject = **I**
   2. Verb = **am going to write**
   3. **I am going to write**... who?/what? = **a letter**
   4. **I am going to write a letter**... to whom?/ for whom? = **you** = Indirect Object Noun

Práctica 4.8

1. Carlos **les** pide ayuda <u>a sus amigos</u>.

   Carlos asks his friends for help. (Carlos asks for help to his friends.)

2. Jorge y yo no **te** queremos decir el secreto <u>a ti</u>.

   Jorge and I don't want to say the secret to you.

174

3. Mi familia **os** mandó una invitación <u>a vosotros</u>.

    My family sent you guys an invitation.

4. <u>A mi amiga, Laura,</u> **le** gustan los animales.

    My friend, Laura, likes animals. (Animals are pleasing to my friend Laura.)

5. Ella siempre **le** explica la lección <u>al estudiante</u>.

    She always explains the lesson to the student.

Práctica 4.9

1. ¿Le diste tú el regalo <u>a tu hermano</u> para su cumpleaños? = *Did you give the gift to your brother for his birthday?*

    Sí, (yo) le di el regalo para su cumpleaños. = *Yes, I gave him the gift for his birthday.*

2. ¿Les explicó la maestra la lección <u>a los estudiantes</u>? = *Did the teacher explain the lesson to the students?*

    Sí, la maestra les explicó la lección. = *Yes, the teacher explained the lesson to them.*

3. ¿Vas tú a mandarme la invitación <u>a mí</u>? = *Are you going to send me the invitation?*

    No, no te voy a mandar la invitación. (or) No, no voy a mandarte la invitación. = *No, I'm not going to send you the invitation.*

4. ¿Nos escribiste tú la carta <u>a mi mamá y a mí</u>? = *Did you write the letter to my mom and to me?*

    No, (yo) no os escribí la carta. (or) No, (yo) no les escribí la carta. = *No, I didn't write the letter to you guys/you all.*

5. ¿Les di yo los documentos <u>a Uds.?</u> = *Did I give the documents to you all?*

    Sí, (tú) nos diste los documentos. = *Yes, you gave us the documents.*

6. ¿Te entrego la tarea <u>a ti</u>? = *Do I turn the homework in to you?*

    Sí, (tú) me entregas la tarea. = *Yes, you turn the homework in to me.*

Práctica 4.10

1. La estudiante <u>le</u> entrega (la tarea) <u>a la maestra</u>. = *The student turns the homework in to the teacher.*

    La estudiante se la entrega. = *The student turns it in to her.*

2. Yo te doy (el regalo) a ti. = *I give the gift to you.*
   Yo te lo doy. = *I give it to you.*

3. Mis padres me compran (el carro) nuevo a mí. = *My parents buy me a new car.*
   Mis padres me lo compran. = *My parents buy it for me.*

4. Uds. nos leen (la historia) a nosotros. = *You all read the story to us.*
   Uds nos la leen. = *You all read it to us.*

5. Nosotros os mandamos (la invitación) a vosotros. = *We are sending the invitation to you guys.*
   Nosotros os la mandamos. = *We are sending it to you guys.*

6. La maestra les explica (la lección) a los estudiantes. = *The teacher explains the lesson to the students.*
   La maestra se la explica. = *The teacher explains it to them.*

Práctica 4.11

1. ¿Le das (besos) a tu esposo/a? = *Do you give your spouse kisses?*
   Se los doy…. = *I give him/her them…*

2. ¿Te compra tu esposo/a (los regalos) a ti? = *Does your spouse buy gifts for you?*
   Mi esposo/a me los da… = *My spouse gives them to me…*

3. ¿Le preparas tú (la cena) a tu familia? = *Do you prepare dinner for your family?*
   Se la preparo …. *I prepare it for them…*

4. ¿Te escribe tu esposo/a (los poemas) a ti? = *Does your spouse write poems for you?*
   Mi esposo/a me los escribe … = *My husband writes them for me …*

5. ¿Les dices tú (los secretos) a tus amigos? = *Do you tell secrets to your friends?*
   Se los digo … = *I tell them to them …*

6. ¿Les das tú (tu ropa vieja) a las organizaciones caricativas (charities)? = *Do you give clothing to charities?*
   Se la doy … = *I give it to them…*

7. ¿Les cuentas tú (los chistes) a tus amigos? = *Do you tell jokes to your friends?*
   Se los cuento… = *I tell them to them ….*

8. ¿Te dan tus padres (consejos) (advice)? = *Do your parents give you advice?*
   Mis padres me los dan … = *My parents give it to me…*

9. ¿Les das tú (los consejos) a tus hijos o a tus amigos? = *Do you give advice to your kids and friends?*
   Se les doy …. = *I give it to them…*

10. ¿Les traes tú (comida) a tus amigos cuando vas a una fiesta en su casa? = *Do you bring food to your friends when you go to a party at their house?*
    Yo se la traigo cuando voy a una fiesta en su casa. = *I bring it to them when I go to a party at their house.*

Práctica 4.12

Ejemplo #1:
Estudiante A: Do you have a pen in your backpack?
Estudiante B: Yes, I have it. I am giving it to you.
Estudiante A: Thank you for giving it to me.

Ejemplo #2
Estudiante B: Do you have a dictionary in your backpack?
Estudiante A: No, I don't have it. I can't give it to you.
Estudiante B: Did you bring a sheet of paper?
Estudiante A: Yes, I brought it. I am giving it to you.

Ejemplo #3
Estudiante A: Can you give me my pen?
Estudiante B: Yes, I'm giving it to you.
Estudiante A: Thank you for returning it to me.

Práctica 4.13
1. *Where are the two people?*
   Las dos personas están en un restaurante. = *The two people are in a restaurant.*

2. *What is there on the table?*
   Hay un mantel, una hielera, champaña y candaleros con velas en la mesa. = *There is a table cloth, an ice bucket, champagne, and candlesticks with candles on the table.*

3. *What is the man giving to the woman?*
   El hombre le da un anillo. = *The man is giving her a ring.*

4. *Why is the man kneeling?*

El hombre se arrodilla porque le va a proponer a la mujer. = *The man is kneeling because he is going to propose to the woman.*

5. *Is the restaurant elegant or simple? How do you know?*

Es un restaurante elegante. Hay champaña y un mantel en la mesa. = *They are in an elegant restaurant. There is champagne and a tablecloth on the table.*

6. *Are there flowers on the table?*

No, no hay flores en la mesa. = *No, there are not any flowers on the table.*

7. *Do you believe that the woman is going to say "yes" or "no" to him? Why?*

Creo que le va a decir "sí". = *I think that she is going to say "yes" to him.*
Creo que le va a decir "no". = *I think she's going to say "no" to him.*
(*Answers will vary as to why.*)

8. *Do you believe that the two are going to eat or have they just finished eating?*

Los dos van a comer. = *The two are going to eat.*

9. *What are they going to drink to celebrate?*

Van a tomar champaña para celebrar. = *They are going to drink champagne to celebrate.*

10. *How much is this night going to cost the man?*

Le va a costar los ahorros de la vida. = *It's going to cost him his life's savings.* ☺

Práctica 4.14

1. *What is the family celebrating? How do you know?*

La familia celebra el cumpleaños de la chica. Hay globos y el mesero le trae torta/pastel de cumpleaños. = *The family is celebrating the girl's birthday. There are balloons and the waiter is bringing a birthday cake.*

2. *Are they going to eat the main dish/course or did they just finish eating it?*

Acaban de comer el plato principal. = *They just finished eating the main dish/course.*

3. *Where are they? Are they in a house or in a restaurant? How do you know?*

Están en un restaurante porque hay un mesero. = *They are in a restaurant because there is a waiter.*

4. *What is the man bringing to the people seated at the table?*

   El hombre les trae una torta/un pastel de cumpleaños. = *The man is bringing a birthday cake.*

5. *Who is the man with the cake? Is he the uncle or the waiter?*

   Él es el mesero. = *He is the waiter.*

6. *Are the people at the table dejected or excited?*

   Las personas en la mesa están emocionadas. = *The people at the table are excited.*

7. *Did the parents bring gifts for the girl?*

   No, los padres no le trajeron regalos. = *No, the parents didn't bring gifts for her.*

8. *Are the candles on the cake lit?*

   Sí, las velas en el pastel están encendidas. = *Yes, the candles on the cake are lit.*

9. *Do you believe that the birthday girl is going to make a wish?*

   Sí creo que la cumpleañera va a pedir un deseo. = *Yes, I think the birthday girl is going to make a wish.*

   No, no creo que la cumpleañera va a pedir un deseo. = *No, I don't think the birthday girl is going to make a wish.*

10. *How old will the birthday girl be?*

    La cumpleañera cumple doce años. = *The birthday girl will be twelve years old.*

Práctica 5.1

1. (Yo) me escribo una carta.
2. Ella se vio en el espejo.
3. (Nosotros) nos hablamos en español.
4. ¿Te amas?
5. Él se oye.

Práctica 5.2

1. *Is it morning or evening in the drawing? How do you know?*

   Es de la mañana. El niño se cepilla los dientes. Todos se preparan. = *It's morning. The little boy is brushing his teeth. Everyone is getting ready/preparing themselves.*

2. *In the bedroom, is the little boy dressing himself or is the dad dressing him?*

   En el dormitorio, el papá lo viste al niño . = *In the bedroom, the dad is dressing the little boy.*

3. *What are the people in the bathroom doing? Do you think the little boy shaved or not?*
   En el baño, el niño se cepilla los dientes. La mujer le peina el pelo de la niña. El niño no se afeitó porque es joven. = *In the bathroom, the boy is brushing his teeth. The woman is combing the girl's hair. The boy didn't shave because he is young.*

4. *What is the woman in the living room doing?*
   La mujer en la sala se mira en el espejo. = *The woman in the living room is looking at herself in the mirror.*

5. *Who is serving breakfast to the kids?*
   La mujer (La mamá) les sirve el desayuno a los niños. = *The woman (mom) is serving the breakfast to the kids.*

6. *Do you think the boy seated to the right of the table is going to give his food to the cat?*
   Answers will vary

Práctica 5.3

1. *Is it morning or evening in the drawing? How do you know?*
   Es de la noche en el dibujo porque todos hacen actividades que las personas hacen por las noches. Se baña, apaga la luz, descansa, etc.. = *It's the evening because everyone is doing activities that people do in the evenings. Someone is bathing, someone turns off the light, someone rests, etc..*

2. *What is the person in the bathroom doing?*
   Ella se baña en el baño. = *She is bathing in the bathroom.*

3. *Why is the boy kneeling in the bedroom? Is he going to propose or is he saying prayers to God?*
   El niño se arrodilla porque le reza a Dios. = *The boy is kneeling because he is praying to God.*

4. *Why is the mom in the room?*
   Answers will vary.

5. *What is the man on the armchair doing in the living room? Is he watching the television program?*
   El hombre lee el periódico. Él no mira el programa en la televisión. = *The man is reading the newspaper. He is not watching the television program?*

6. *Is the man in the kitchen turning the light off or on? What is the man going to do?*
    El hombre en la cocina apaga la luz. Va a acostarse. = *The man in the kitchen is turning off the light. He is going to go to bed.*

Práctica 5.4
For Reader A

1. *What is the name of the main character of the story? Is her name Yolanda or Oliviana?*
    La personaje principal se llama Oliviana. = *The main character's name is Oliviana.*

2. *What is she like? Is she hardworking or lazy?*
    Ella es trabajadora. = *She is hard-working.*

3. *Where did Oliviana stay?*
    Ella se alojó en un hotel muy elegante en Punta Cana. = *She stayed in a very elegant hotel in Punta Cana.*

4. *Did Oliviana go to bed late the first night in the hotel?*
    No. Se acostó temprano la primera noche en el hotel. – *No. She went to bed early the first night in the hotel.*

5.   *Why didn't Oliviana fall asleep until very late?*
    No se durmió Oliviana hasta muy tarde porque la familia que se alojaba en el cuarto al lado del cuarto de ella hablaba en voces altas toda la noche.   Los niños se peleaban y los padres les gritaban. = *Oliviana didn't fall asleep until very late because the family staying in the room next to hers was talking in loud voices all night. The kids were fighting and the parents were shouting at them.*

6. *Oliviana didn't set the alarm clock, but what other reason is there for not waking up on time in the morning?*
    Oliviana no pudo dormirse hasta muy tarde. = *Oliviana couldn't fall asleep until very late.*

7. *At what time did Oliviana wake up?*
    Se despertó a las nueve y media. = *She woke up at 9:30.*

8. *At what time did the office meeting start?*
    La reunión de la oficina empezó a las ocho. = *The office meeting started at 8:00.*

9. *Where were all her colleagues when Olviana met up/found them?*

Todos sus colegas estaban en la piscina del hotel cuando Oliviana se encontró con ellos.

= All her colleagues were in the hotel pool when Oliviana met up with them.

10. *Why did Oliviana realize that sometimes it's better to arrive late?*

Porque puede divertirse más. *= Because she can enjoy herself more.*

Práctica 5.4
For Reader B:

1. *Where did Jorge go?*

Jorge fue a Aguascalientes, México. *= Jorge went to Aguascalientes, Mexico.*

2. *In which month did he travel? Do you remember the specific date?*

Viajó en el mes de noviembre. Viajó el primero de noviembre. *= He traveled in the month of November. He traveled on November 1.*

3. *Did Jorge arrive in the morning or evening?*

Jorge llegó tarde en la noche. *= Jorge arrived late at night.*

4. *Upon arriving at the hotel was Jorge going to go to bed or get up?*

Al llegar al hotel, iba a acostarse. *= Upon arriving to the hotel, he was going to go to bed.*

5. *What did Jorge see when he arrived to the street?*

Jorge vio un montón de colores bonitos y muchas personas. Vio los esqueletos bailando en las calles *= Jorge saw a ton of pretty colors and many people. He saw skeletons dancing in the streets.*

6. *What did Jorge think when the people were celebrating?*

Jorge creía que las personas celebraban la noche de brujas. *= Jorge thought the people were celebrating Halloween.*

7. *n reality, what were they celebrating?*

En realidad celebraban el día de los muertos. *= In reality they were celebrating the Day of the Dead.*

8. *They say that on the Day of the Dead the people use skeletons and masks to make fun of death. What did Jorge see that corresponds to this idea?*
Los esqueletos eran cómicos. = *The skeletons were funny.*

9. *What is the painting "La Catrina" like and who painted it?*
Es una pintura famosa de José Guadalupe Posada y muchas personas usan esta pintura y calavera para representar las ideas del día de los muertos. En la pintura la calavera lleva un sombrero elegante porque La Catrina representa y se burla de los ricos. = *It's a painting by José Guadalupe Posada and many people use this painting and skull to represent the ideas of Day of the Dead. In the painting the skull wears an elegant hat because La Catrina represents and mocks the rich.*

10. *What were the families in the cemetery doing?*
Las familias decoraban los altares. = *The families were decorating the altars.*

Práctica 6.1
1. Eat many vegetables.

2. Exercise.

3. Participate in activities that make you happy.

4. Spend time with friends or family.

5. Continue learning.

Práctica 6.2
1. Llega al trabajo a tiempo. = *Arrive to work on time.*

2. Ten cuidado con tu trabajo. = *Be careful with your work.*

3. Escucha las instrucciones. = *Listen to the instructions.*

4. Pon todos los documentos en un lugar seguro. = *Put all documents in a safe place.*

5. Haz preguntas y di la verdad. = *Ask questions and tell the truth.*

6. Conoce a los secretarios y a tus colegas. = *Meet/Become familiar with the secretaries and your colleagues.*

Práctica 6.3
1. Tome el vaso. (Take the glass)

2. Coman y disfruten. (Eat and enjoy)

3. No salgas. (Don't leave)

4. Abramos los regalos. (Let's open the gifts)

5. No haga el trabajo ahora. (Don't do work now)

Práctica 6.4

1. No llegues tarde.

2. Almuerce conmigo.

3. Busquen mis llaves.

4. Paguemos la cuenta.

5. No crucen la calle.

Práctica 6.5

1. No pidamos pizza.

2. Repitamos el vocabulario nuevo.

3. No nos acostemos.

4. Almorcemos en el restaurante.

5. Empecemos temprano.

6. No sigamos las reglas.

7. No compitamos.

8. Ríamos mucho.

Práctica 6.6

1. Sepan de memoria el vocabulario de este libro. = *Memorize the vocabulary from this book.*

2. No vaya al trabajo durante las vacaciones. = *Don't go to work during vacation.*

3. No les des las drogas a los niños. = *Don't give drugs to kids.*

4. No seamos antipáticos. = *Let's not be mean.*

5. No estés en la piscina mientras truena. = *Don't be in the pool while it's thundering.*

6. Estén felices = *Be happy.*

Práctica 6.7

1. No escriba con la mano izquierda. = Don't *write with your left hand.*

2. Escriba con la mano derecha. = *Write with your right hand.*

3. No se mueva la muñeca. = *Don't move your wrist.*

4. Báñese con la venda. = *Bathe with the bandage.*

   (or) No se bañe con la venda. = *Don't bathe with the bandage.*

5. No conduzca un coche por una larga distancia. = *Don't drive a car for a long distance.*

6. No practique el boxeo. = *Don't practice boxing.*

7. Tenga cuidado. = *Be careful.*

8. Mantenga limpia la venda. = *Keep the bandage clean.*

9. Visite la clínica en seis semanas. = *Visit the clinic in six weeks.*

10. No ande en las montañas rusas. = *Don't ride on roller coasters.*

Práctica 6.8

1. Juan, dénoslo.

2. Sr. Arroyo, por favor muéstremela.

3. Jorge y Manuel, no nos lo digan.

4. Sr. y Sra. Martínez, siéntense por favor.

5. ¡Vayamos a la playa!

6. Carlitos, no lo toques.

7. Mamá, no me lo hagas.

8. No nos peleemos.

9. Verónica, léemela.

10. Amigos, no me los compren.

Práctica 6.9

1. *Can I lift weights?*
      No, no las levante. = *No, don't lift them.*

2. *Can I go to the gym?*
      Sí, vaya al gimnasio. = *Yes, go to the gym.*

3. *Should I lie down and sleep on the ground?*
   No, no se acueste ni duerma en el suelo. = *No, don't lie down or sleep on the ground.*

4. *Can I ride on fast roller coasters?*
   No, no ande en las montañas rusas y rápidas. = *No don't ride on roller coasters.*

5. *Can I put ice on?*
   Sí, póngaselo. = *Yes, put it on.*

6. *Can I run through the streets?*
   No, no corra por las calles. = *No don't run through the streets.*

7. *Can I go shopping?*
   Sí, vaya de compras. = *Yes, go shopping.*

8. *Can I wear really tall heels?*
   No, no los lleve. = *No, don't wear them.*

Práctica 6.10

1. No corras en la calle. = *Don't run in the street* = Nicolás

2. Come muchas verduras. = *Eat many vegetables.* = Pablo

3. No comas dulces. = *Don't eat candy/sweets.* = Pedro

4. Acuéstate temprano. = *Go to bed early* = Natalie

5. Póngase derecho. No se encorve. = *Stand up straight. Don't slouch.* = Señor Estrada

6. Lleve los zapatos confortables. = *Wear comfortable shoes.* = Señora Cruz

Práctica 6.11

1.   a. ¡Comamos en un restaurante mexicano!
        b. ¡Vamos a comer en un restaurante mexicano!
        c. ¡A comer en un restaurante mexicano!
2.   a. ¡Miremos una película!
        b. ¡Vamos a mirar una película!
        c. ¡A mirar una película!
3.   a. ¡Caminemos al parque!
        b. ¡Vamos a caminar al parque!
        c. ¡A caminar al parque!

4. a. ¡Practiquemos español!

   b. ¡Vamos a practicar español!

   c. ¡A practicar español!

Práctica 7.1

1. S - (influence)

2. S – (emotion)

3. I - (certainty, no doubt)

4. S - (doubt)

5. S - (doubt)

6. I - (no doubt)

7. S - (influence)

8. I – (no doubt)

9. S – (emotion)

10. I - (no change of subject!)

11. S – (emotion)

12. I - (no change of subject)

13. S - (influence)

14. I - (statement; no influence)

15. S - (influence)

16. S - (influence)

17. S - (influence)

18. S - (speculation; contrary-to-fact)

19. I - (influence)

20. I - (no doubt)

21. I - (no doubt)

22. I - (the trigger verb is in the indicative)

23. S - (emotion)

24. I - (no doubt)

25. I - (statement of fact; no doubt)

26. I - (no doubt)

27. S - (influence)

28. S - (influence)

29. S - (doubt)

30. I - (no change of subject)

31. S - (emotion)

32. S - (speculation)

33. I - (no doubt)

34. S - (speculation; we may not find anyone)

35. S - (speculation)

36. S - (doubt)

Práctica 7.2

1. El jefe no quiere que sus empleados **usen** sus teléfonos celulares en la oficina.
   The boss doesn't want his employees to use their cell phones in the office.

2. No me gusta que tú **trabajes** hasta muy tarde por la noche.
   I don't like that you work until very late at night.

3. Ojalá que Uds. **hagan** todo el trabajo hoy.
   I hope that (God willing) you all do all the work today.

4. Es importante que los empleados **sigan** todas las instrucciones.
   It's important that the employees follow all the instructions.

5. El jefe nos dice que nosotros **escribamos** los reportes ahora.
   The boss tells us to write the reports now.

6. La compañía prohíbe que los clientes **vean** los documentos de otros clientes.
   The company prohibits clients from seeing other clients' documents.

7. Los empleados no hacen el trabajo hasta que el jefe se lo **mande**.
   The employees don't do the work until the boss demands them to do it.

8. Ellos quieren que nosotros **pongamos** los documentos completos en los archivos.
   They want us to put the completed documents in the files.

9. Dudo que los clientes **tengan** tanto éxito con otra compañía.
   I doubt that the clients will have as much success with another company.

10. Es importante que todos **conozcan** bien a su jefe y a sus empleados.
    It's important that everyone knows their boss and his employees.

Práctica 7.3

1. Ojalá que Uds. **lleguen** a tiempo.
   I hope that (God willing) you all arrive on time.

2. Dudamos que los empleados **almuercen** en la cafetería.
   We doubt that the employees have lunch in the cafeteria.

3. No creo que el jefe **busque** los reportes.
   I don't believe the boss is looking for the reports.

4. Es preferido que tú **entregues** los documentos temprano.
   It's preferable that you turn the documents in early.

5. Los clientes esperan que Uds. **comiencen** inmediatamente.
   The clients hope that you all begin immediately.

6. A los clientes les gusta cuando nosotros **toquemos** música.
   The clients/customers like when we play music.

Práctica 7.4

1. Es importante que los empleados nunca **mientan**.
   It's important that the employees never lie.

2. Ojalá que los clientes **entiendan** las instrucciones.
   I hope (God willing) the clients understand the instructions.

3. Nuestro jefe prefiere que nosotros **empecemos** ahora.
   Our boss prefers that we begin now.

4. Mi cliente quiere que yo **pida** su permiso antes de hacer decisiones importantes.
   My client wants me to ask permission before making important decisions.

5. Mi colega y yo esperamos que el jefe **repita** las instrucciones.
   My colleague and I hope the boss repeats the instructions.

6. Ojalá que mis colegas y yo no **nos riamos** durante la presentación.
   I hope that my colleagues and I don't laugh during the presentation.

7. Es importante que todos los empleados **se vistan** de ropa profesional.
   It's important that all the employees dress in professional clothing.

Práctica 7.5

1. The boy wants the swimmer to rescue him. = Verdad
2. The fisherman hopes that the boy doesn't scare the fish. = Verdad
3. At the beach it is prohibited that the dogs enter the beach. = Falso
4. The rules on the beach prohibit fishermen from eating the fish. = Falso
5. The people that are sitting under the umbrella want it to be very hot. = Falso
6. The people under the umbrella want the dog to bark. = Falso
7. The boy wants the fisherman to see him. = Verdad
8. The fisherman wants the dog not to bark much. = Verdad

Práctica 7.6

A	B
1. I doubt that my friends go to the beach today.	1. I doubt that my friends are giving me a gift today.
2. In my opinion, it is important that the students are friendly.	2. In my opinion, it's important that everyone arrive on time to class.
3. My friends always want me to be happy.	3. My friends want me to always know the answers.

4. I don't believe that the teachers give too much homework in school.	4. In general, I don't believe that doctors are friendly.
5. I doubt that it is going to rain a lot this winter.	5. I prefer that no one gives me gifts for my birthday.
6. It's better that the young people don't know anything about the financial matters of the family.	6. It's preferable that the young people know how to drive a stick shift (manual transmission) of a car.

Práctica 7.7

1. The mom and the cat are sleeping on the couch. = verdad

2. The mom is having a bad dream. = Falso

3. The mom wants the people from her family to do the chores of the house. = verdad

4. The mom wants a person from the family to wash the dishes. = verdad

5. In her dream, the mom wants a person to take her to the beach. = falso

6. In her dream, the mom hopes that a person will sweep the floor. = verdad

7. The cat wants the mom to work more. = falso

8. Actually, the mom doubts that the other people are going to help her in the house. = verdad

9. It's probable that the mom is going to do all the chores in the house. = verdad

10. It's evident that mom always does the chores in the house. = verdad

11. The cat also has a dream. = verdad

12. The cat wants the dog to stay in its cage. = verdad

Práctica 7.8

Answers may vary, but might include the following:
1. "It's important that you all take off your shoes before entering." = en la casa de un amigo
2. "I hope that they accept credit cards here" – un restaurante o un parque de atracciones
3. "I doubt that the player is going to score a goal" = en un partido de fútbol
4. "It's prohibited that we touch the paintings and sculptures". = en un museo
5. "It's necessary that you all put the carry-on luggage in the luggage rack." = en el avión
6. "I recommend that you wear sandals instead of tennis shoes." = en la playa
7. "We are glad that the animals are happy here." = en el zoológico
8. "They deny that the roller coaster is dangerous." = En un parque de atracciones

9. "It's necessary that you show identification." = en el aeropuerto/ en un banco
10. "Im not sure that he is paying the bill." = en la primera cita
11. "It's better that you don't use the dictionary." = en una clase de español
12. "It's necessary that we find a room with two large beds." = en un hotel
13. "I recommend that you speak with clients with much patience and courtesy" = en la oficina, hotel, o en un restaurante
14. "I'm glad that they serve vegetarian meals here." = en un restaurante
15. "I ask that you all form a line before boarding." = en el aeropuerto
16. "I hope that they play my favorite song." = en un concierto
17. "I hope the tiger can't escape from his cage." = en el zoológico
18. "I'll introduce you to my family when we know each other better." = en la primera cita

Práctica 8.1

Infinitive	3rd Person Plural Preterite	Imperfect Subjunctive
1. vivir	**vivieron**	Yo **viviera**
2. divertirse	**se divirtieron**	Tú **te diviertieras**
3. ser	**fueron**	Ud. **fuera**
4. ir	**fueron**	Él **fuera**
5. venir	**vinieron**	Nosotros **viniéramos**
6. hacer	**hicerion**	Vosotros **hicierais**
7. sentarse	**se sentaron**	Ellos **se sentaran**
8. reírse	**se rieron**	Uds. **se rieran**
9. pagar	**pagaron**	Yo **pagara**
10. dormir	**durmieron**	Nosotros **durmiéramos**
11. traer	**trajeron**	Tú **trajeras**
12. mentir	**mintieron**	Ella **mintiera**

Práctica 8.2

1. El seguridad quería que los pasajeros del avión **se quitaran** los zapatos antes de abordar el avión.

   The security wanted the passengers of the plane to take off their shoes before boarding the plane.

2. El entrevistador le preguntó al actor en una manera de que el actor no **pudiera** mentir.

   The interviewer asked the actor questions in a way that the actor couldn't lie.

3. Yo te la expliqué para que tú **entendieras** la situación.

   I explained it to you so that you would understand the situation.

4. Ellos no creían que nosotros **conociéramos** al diplomático de ese país.

   They didn't believe that we knew the diplomat from that country.

5. El intérprete habló lentamente para que nosotros **siguiéramos** escuchando la conversación.

   The interpreter spoke slowly so we would continue listening to the conversation.

6. Mi amiga esperaba que yo **trajera** las bebidas a su fiesta.

   My friend hoped that I would bring the drinks to her party.

7. El jefe del negocio buscaba a una persona que **hablara** español e inglés.

   The boss of the business was looking for a person who spoke Spanish and English.

8. Mi novio no iba a ir a Aguascalientes a menos que yo **fuera** con él.

   My boyfriend wasn't going to go to Aguascalientes unless I went with him.

9. Yo no pude dormirme hasta que mi esposo **volviera**.

   I couldn't fall asleep until my husband returned.

10. Era dudoso que los estudiantes **estuvieran** contentos después de aprender las reglas del subjuntivo.

    It was doubtful that the students were happy after learning the rules of the subjunctive.

Práctica 8.3

1. Ellos no permitieron que nosotros **saliéramos**.

   They didn't permit us to leave.

2. La maestra esperaba que los estudiantes **entendieran** la lección.

   The teacher hoped that the students understood the lesson.

3. Era probable que ellos **vieran** la película ayer.
   It was probable that they saw the movie yesterday.

4. Es probable que ella ya **sepa** las respuestas.
   It's probable that she already knows the answers.

5. Me alegro de que Uds. **estén** aquí esta noche.
   I'm glad that you are all here tonight.

6. Ella no creía que yo **fuera** presidente del club.
   She didn't believe that I was president of the club.

7. Yo dudo que él **pague** la cuenta.
   I doubt that he is paying the bill.

8. Ella dudaba que él **conociera** a Brad Pitt.
   She doubted that he knew Brad Pitt.

9. Uds. se alegran de que nosotros **hablemos** en español.
   You all are glad that we speak in Spanish.

10. Es importante que nosotros **escuchemos** las instrucciones cuidadosamente.
    It is important that we listen to the instructions carefully.

11. Te recomendé que (ellos) **fueran** al Museo Nacional.
    I recommended to you that they go to the National Museum.

12. La maestra nos recomienda que (nosotros) **estudiemos** el vocabulario cada día.
    The teacher recommends that we study the vocabulary every day.

13. Yo no creía que tú **quisieras** hacer el trabajo.
    I didn't believe that you wanted to do the work.

14. Tú dudabas que yo **comiera** comida exótica.
    You doubted that I ate exotic food.

Práctica 8.4

Preguntas
1. Did your parents insist that you do your homework immediately after returning from school?
2. Did you want your parents to give you more freedom?
3. Did you study only so a university would accept you?
4. Did you doubt that the classes were important for your future?
5. Was it more important that you spend time with friends or with your family?
6. Did you like when your friends came to your house or did you prefer that your friends invite you to their houses?
7. Did your parents suggest that you participate in school activities?
8. Did your parents permit that you sleep at friends' houses?
9. Did you leave the house without your parents' knowing?
10. Did your friends insist that you keep their secrets?
11. Did your parents advise you to study more, sleep more, or that you have more fun?
12. Did you doubt that your friends always told you the truth?
13. Did you prefer that your parents advise you or that they leave you alone to make your own decisions?
14. Were you afraid that no one liked you?

Práctica 8.5

There once was a very unpleasant boss. (1. Was the man a boss or an employee?) The boss's name was Jorge Gruñón. He was the owner of a very popular magazine. (2. Was Jorge Gruñón owner of a newspaper or of a magazine?) Mr. Gruñón always wanted his employees to do a lot of work. (3. Did the boss give a lot or a little work to his employees?) The employees weren't bothered that the boss gave them a lot of work. What bothered them was that Mr. Gruñón asked them to do unimportant work. (4. Do the employees have problems with the idea of doing a lot of work? Was the work that the boss gave them important?)

For example, one day Mr. Gruñón arrived to the office and asked Susana, a very talented employee, to bring him coffee. (5. Did the boss want Susana to bring him tea or coffee?) But he didn't want coffee from the coffee maker in the office. Of course not. Mr. Gruñón demanded that Susana go to Starbucks to buy him special coffee. He preferred the coffee from Starbucks because he believed that it was more delicious.

(6. Was Mr. Gruñón content with the coffee from the office? Where did he want Susana to go to buy his coffee?) Susana graduated from the university and had a bachelors degree in photography. (7. Was Susan an employee without or with talent?) She graduated with honors from the university. She was a photographer and she did not like to run errands for her boss. (8. Did Susana accept the job at the magazine to run errands for the boss or to take photos?) Anyway, she did it because she wanted to be a photographer for the magazine.

Another day Mr. Gruñón asked Pablo, a marvelous writer, to take his dirty clothes to the laundry. (9. Is Pablo a waiter or a writer? Did Mr. Gruñón want Pablo to write an article or to take his clothes to the laundry?) Pablo was angry that the boss asked him to do a chore so useless, but he took the clothes to the laundry. (10. Did Pablo write an article or did he take the clothing?) Pablo believed that in the future, the boss would ask him to write an article for the magazine. (11. Did Pablo believe that he was going to write an article for the magazine in the future?)

And the poor editor, Alisa… Mr. Gruñón asked her to pick up his kids from the school. (12. Did Alisa have to pick up her own kids from the school or Mr. Gruñón's kids?) This chore was the worst of all because Mr. Gruñón's kids were terrible. They always shouted and begged Alisa to buy them ice cream and other sweets. But Alisa never would buy them for them. (13. Did Mr. Gruñón's kids behave well or badly? Did Alisa buy them sweets?)

Mr. Gruñón's life was good, but the employees were sad. (14. Were the employees happy or angry?) But one day, while Susana was in Starbucks, she took a photo of a man. The man saw the photo, and he offered Susana a job with his magazine. (15. Who took the photo? Did the man like the photo? What did he offer Susana? Did Susana want to work for the other company?) Susana told the man that she knew two fantastic employees – a writer and an editor. She asked her new boss to offer them a job. (16. Did Susana want her new boss to offer more money or a position with the company to them?) The man said that he preferred that his photographers work with people of their preference. And so it was that they two left together to speak with Alisa and Pablo. (17. Do you believe that Alisa and Pablo are going to accept the job with this new magazine?)

Práctica 8.6

There was a traveler that always traveled through the Spanish speaking world. (1. Did the woman travel to countries where they spoke French or Spanish?) Her name was Carolina. (2. What was the traveler's name?) Carolina loved to travel, but she wasn't a very nice traveler. She was rude and selfish. (3. Was Carolina nice with other people from the other countries?)

For example, when Carolina was in other countries where they didn't speak English, she insisted that the natives of that country speak to her in English. (4. What language did Carolina speak? What language did Carolina want the native people to speak?) The native people got angry generally, but they tried to speak in English to communicate with Carolina. The native people didn't' want Carolina to be unhappy with her visit. (5. Did the native people want to speak English? Did they want Carolina to be happy? What language did the native people speak with Carolina?)

One day while Carolina was traveling through Mexico, she decided to go shopping in a market full of fresh vegetables. (6. Did Carolina want to buy clothing or vegetables?) She wanted to buy some peppers because she knew that the peppers from Mexico were delicious and unique. (7. Did she want to buy tomatoes or peppers? Did she want peppers because they are spicy/hot or because they are delicious?) Carolina began to speak with the lady selling peppers. (8. Do you believe that Carolina spoke with the saleswoman in English or in Spanish?) As usual, Carolina began to speak with the woman in English. The saleswoman answered her in Spanish. (9. Did Carolina want the saleswoman to speak to her in English or in Spanish?) Carolina insisted that the saleswoman speak in English, but the saleswoman didn't speak English. She spoke Spanish. (10. Why didn't the saleswoman speak English – because she didn't want to or because she only spoke Spanish?) Carolina said to the saleswoman, "I would like for you to speak to me in English. I am not going to buy anything unless you speak to me in English." (11. If the saleswoman speaks Spanish, is Carolina going to buy the peppers? Can the saleswoman speak English?) And the woman responded, "I don't speak English. And we are in Mexico. Please, I beg that you speak to me in Spanish." (12. Does the saleswoman want Carolina to buy the peppers from her?)

Carolina got angry and said to the woman that she didn't like that the woman didn't understand English. Carolina went to the store that was immediately to the right. (13. Where did Carolina go... to a store very far away or a very close store?) That saleswoman heard and saw everything between Carolina and the other woman. (14. Did the new saleswoman listen to the conversation between Carolina and the other saleswoman?) Carolina told the saleswoman there that she would like to buy peppers from her if she spoke in English. (15. Does the saleswoman from the store to the right understand or not understand English?)

Carolina asked in English that the woman give her some delicious and unique peppers – the most delicious and unique of all. (16. Did Carolina ask for fresh and sweet peppers or delicious and unique peppers?) The saleswoman smiled and gave her a bag full of peppers. In English the saleswoman said to Carolina, "I chose the best peppers for you." (17. Did Carolina choose the peppers?)

Carolina walked to the park to eat some of the peppers. (18. Why did Carolina walk to the park... to read or to eat?) When she arrived there, she sat down on a bench and opened the bag. She was surprised that the woman had put only old and rotten peppers in the bag. (19. Did the saleswoman choose good or bad peppers?) There was only one good pepper in the bag. (20. Were all the peppers bad?) Carolina took the one out and took a bite. (21. Did Carolina eat a part or not any part of the pepper?) It was so spicy that she felt as if there were a fire in her mouth! She couldn't eat a single bite more. (22. Could Carolina eat the pepper? Do you belive the saleswoman chose the spiciest pepper? Did the saleswoman want to teach Carolina a lesson?) From that moment on, Carolina didn't insist that others speak English. (23. Did Carolina learn a lesson from this experience?) She decided to take Spanish classes to speak with people in Spanish. (24. What was the result of her experience? What is Carolina going to do?)

Práctica 8.7

1. *Why was the mom of the young girl angry?*
   La mamá no estaba contenta de que su hija siempre usara su teléfono celular en vez de hablar con ella.
   The mom wasn't happy that her daughter was always using her cell pone instead of talking with her.

2. *Why didn't the young girl smile at her mom?*
   No quería levantarse para que su mamá pudiera sentarse en la silla al lado de ella.
   She didn't want to get up so that her mom could sit down in the chair next to her.

3. *What did the little boy that was grabbing at his mom's skirt want?*
   Quería que su mamá lo llevara al baño.
   He wanted his mom to take him to the bathroom.

4. *What did the little boy's mom want?*
   Quería que la empleada de la línea aérea le diera su tarjeta de embarque.
   She wanted the airline employee to give her her boarding pass.

5. *Why did the employee have a microphone in her hand?*
   Quería que la gente formaran una cola para abordar el avión.
   She wanted the people to form a line to board the plane.

6. *Why was the man with the suitcase looking at the clocks?*
   No creía que su avión llegara tarde porque no sabía qué hora era.
   He didn't believe that his plane arrived late because he didn't know what time it was.

197

7. *Why was the man with the cell phone in a bad mood?*
   Quería que su esposa contestara el teléfono para que pudiera hablar con ella.
   He wanted his wife to answer the telephone so he might be able to speak with her.

8. *Why was the employee smiling while all the passengers were complaining and getting angry?*
   Sabía que todos iban a salir dentro de poco tiempo.
   She knew that everyone was going to leave within a short while.

Prática 9.1

Verb Infinitive	Past Participle	English Translation
Hablar	**Hablado**	**Spoken**
Vivir	**Vivido**	**Lived**
Almorzar	**Almorzado**	**Had lunch**
Entender	**Entendido**	**Understood**
Conocer	**Conocido**	**Known**
Aburrir	**Aburrido**	**Bored**
Cerrar	**Cerrado**	**Closed**
Preocupar	**Preocupado**	**Worried**

Práctica 9.2
1. Ella ha recomendado el restaurante mexicano.
2. ¡Nosotros hemos aprendido mucho en esta clase! ☺
3. ¿Vosotros habéis (or Uds. han) visto la película "Macario"?
5. ¡Vosotros habéis (or Uds. han) hecho el trabajo!
6. Carlos, tú has oído las noticias, ¿verdad?
7. Yo no he viajado allí por años.
8. ¿Has estudiado para el examen, Susana?
9. Mis amigos me han visto.
10. Miguel y Rafael han reído toda la noche.

11. ¿Quién te ha dicho esa mentira?

12. ¿Vosotros no habéis escrito (or Uds. no han escrito) la carta?

Práctica 9.3
Answers will vary

Práctica 9.4

My friends and I have done many activities this summer. We have traveled by plane from New York to California. We have spent some days in San Francisco. We have visited some of my friend Katia's relatives. We have already spent some days in Southern California in Los Angeles. Two from our group have visited the Museum of Tolerance. I didn't go with them, but I have gone to the Museum of Natural History. Here in Los Angeles I have seen many interesting places. I have seen people selling rare things on the beach of Venice. I have seen the Santa Monica Pier with all the rides and food stores. But also I have done some marvelous activities here. For example, my friends and I have skated along the path that goes through all the beaches. We have taken a tour on a double-decker bus. We have put our hands in the hand prints of the famous actors of Hollywood. Also we have looked for Hollywood stars, but still we haven't seen a single famous actor. Have you seen some famous people in Hollywood?

Práctica 9.5
1. Who (all) has climbed the Eiffel Tower? (Josefina)
2. Who (all) has had fun adventures? (Todos... Josefina, Marta, Guillermo y Roberto)
3. Who (all) has run with the bulls? (Guillermo)
4. Who (all) has climbed a mountain? (Marta)
5. Who (all) has traveled to Spain? (Guillermo)
6. Who (all) has traveled through South America by bus? (Roberto)
7. Who (all) has been afraid during his/her trip? (Guillermo)
8. Who (all) has traveled to a place where it was cold? (Marta)

Práctica 9.6
1. Who (all) has worked today? (Pablo y Victoria)
2. Who (all) has deposited money in the bank today? (Liana)
3. Who (all) has taught a class today? (Victoria)
4. Who (all) has spent time with friends today? (Carolina)
5. Who (all) has felt frustrated today? (Sarita y Pablo)
6. Who (all) has left from the house today? (Todos – Carolina, Pablo, Liana, Sarita y Victoria)
7. Who (all) has gone shopping today? (Sarita)

8. Who (all) has drawn today? (Pablo)
9. Who (all) has enjoyed him/herself most today? (Carolina)
10. Who (all) has spent too much money today? (Sarita)

Práctica 10.1
1. ¿Quién había leído este capítulo antes de entrar en la clase?
2. Apenas nosotros habíamos abierto la puerta cuando ellos llamaron.
3. Tan pronto como nosotros habíamos llegado, nuestros amigos salieron.
4. Yo no había visto esa película.
5. Mis amigos habían puesto los libros en mi coche.
6. Anita, ¿habías cerrado las ventantas antes de que empezó a llover?
7. ¿Habíais vosotros (or Habían Uds.) abierto las puertas?
8. ¿Habían Uds. cantado la canción?

Práctica 10.2

_____ I had seen the news on the television.

_____ I had spoken with my relatives.

_____ I had brushed my teeth.

_____ I had prepared my lunch for tomorrow.

_____ I had had coffee.

_____ I had spent time with friends.

_____ I had driven a car.

_____ I had listened to music on the radio.

_____ I had paid some bills.

_____ I had spoken on the phone with some friends.

_____ I had bought something new.

_____ I had gone shopping in a clothing store.

_____ I had bought food from the supermarket.

_____ I had read some chapters of a novel.

_____ I had sent a text.

_____ I had studied Spanish.

_____ I had spoken in Spanish with a heritage speaker.

_____ I had organized my house.

Práctica 10.3

1. *Who are the people in the drawing? Do you believe they are all part of the same family?*
   Hay una madre, un padre y una hija en el dibujo. Son parte de la misma familia. = *There is a mother, a father and a daughter in the drawing. They are all part of the same family.*

2. *What had the daughter been doing? How do you know?*
   La hija había bailado. Ella lleva zapatillas de ballet. = *The daughter had danced. She is carrying ballet slippers.*

3. *What had the man done? How do you know?*
   El hombre había trabajado. Lleva un traje. = *The man had worked. He is wearing a suit.*

4. *What had the woman done? How do you know?*
   La mujer había cocido la comida. Hay comida en la mesa y ella la sirve. = *The woman had cooked the meal. There is food on the table and she is serving it.*

5. *Had the man left from work or is he leaving for work?*
   El hombre había salido del trabajo. = *The man had left from work.*

6. *Do you believe that the daughter had had fun? How do you know?*
   La hija se había divertido porque se sonríe. = *The daughter had enjoyed herself because she is smiling.*

7. *Had the man liked his work? How do you know?*
   Al hombre le había gustado el trabajo. Él se sonríe. = *The man had liked his work. He is smiling.*

8. *Had the woman bought or prepared the meal?*
   La mujer había preparado la comida. = *The woman had prepared the meal.*

Práctica 10.4
Answers will vary, but might include some of the following:

1. Sofía había ido al mercado para comprar los ingredientes.
   Sofía had gone to the store to buy the ingredients.

2. Ella había comprado el polvo para hacer pasteles.
   She had bought the cake mix.

3. Sofía había buscado la receta.
   Sofía had looked for the recipe.

4. Había mezclado todos los ingredientes.
   She had mixed all the ingredients.

5. Había puesto la mezcla en la bizcochera.
   She had put he mixture (batter) in the cake tin.

6. Había puesto la bizcochera en el horno.
   She had put the cake tin in the oven.

7. Había horneado el pastel por 20 minutos a los 350 grados.
   She had baked the cake for 20 minutes at 350 degrees.

8. Había sacado el pastel del horno.
   She had taken the cake out of the oven.

9. Había enfriado el pastel.
   She had cooled the cake.

10. Había cubierto el pastel de escarcha.
    She had frosted the cake.

11. Había puesto las velas.
    She had put on the candles.

12. Había encendido las velas y cantado "Feliz cumpleaños".
    She had lit the candles and sung "Happy Birthday".

Práctica 11.1

1. El jefe **requerirá** que los empleados completen el trabajo.
   The boss will require that the employees complete the work.

2. Yo **pagaré** la cuenta.
   I will pay the bill.

3. Los estudiantes **asistirán** a las clases.
   The students will attend the classes.

4. ¿**Estarán** Uds. contentos?
   Will you all be happy?

5. ¿**Venderéis** vosotros los carros viejos?
   Will you guys sell the old cars?

6. Mis amigos y yo **nos sentaremos** en la primera fila en la clase.
   My friends and I will sit in the first row in the class.

7. El doctor **leerá** los resultados.
   The doctor will read the results.

8. ¿**Traerás** tú las empanadas?
   Will you bring the empanadas?

9. **Será** la una de la tarde cuando lleguen.
   It will be 1:00pm when they arrive.

10. Tú y yo **conoceremos** a nuevos amigos.
    You and I will meet new friends.

Práctica 11.2

1. Yo **habré** leído capítulo dos para la próxima clase.
   I will have read chapter two for the next class.

2. Nosotros **querremos** practicar más.
   We will want to practice more.

3. Ana **saldrá** a las ocho de la mañana.
   Ana will leave at 8:00AM.

4. **Habrá** muchos documentos para firmar.
   There will be many documents to sign.

5. Esa escultura **valdrá** mucho dinero.
   That sculpture will be worth a lot of money.

6. Creo que esos libros **cabrán** en el estante para libros.
   I believe those books will fit in the bookshelf.

7. Uds. **habrán** escrito muchas de las palabras.
   You all will have written many of the words.

8. Mi familia **podrá** ir con Uds. al lago.
   My family will be able to go with all of you to the lake.

9. Yo no **sabré** jugar pero yo **podré** mirar el partido.
   I will not know how to play, but I will be able to watch the game.

10. ¿**Tendrás** tú ganas de ir de compras mañana?
    Will you feel like going shopping tomorrow?

Práctica 11.3

(For each "meta" below you'll find the translation of the goal first and then the question you would ask your partner second)

1. I will have more patience with others.
   ¿Tendrás más paciencia con otros?

2. I will lose weight.
   ¿Perderás de peso?

3. I will exercise more.
   ¿Harás más ejercicio?

4. I will gain weight.
   ¿Ganarás de peso?

5. I will eat healthier food.
   ¿Comerás comida más saludable?

6. I will spend more time with family and friends.
   ¿Pasarás más tiempo con tu familia y amigos?

7. I will save money.
   ¿Ahorrarás dinero?

8. I will work more.
   ¿Trabajarás más?

9. I will travel to another country.
   ¿Viajarás a otro país?

10. I will look for a new job.
     ¿Buscarás empleo nuevo?

Práctica 11.4

1. *Who are the people in the picture? How do you know?*
   Una mujer es adivina. Lleva un turbante. La mujer en la otra silla es cliente porque quiere que la adivina le diga información sobre su futuro. = *One woman is a fortune-teller. She is wearing a turban. The woman in the other chair is a customer because she wants the fortune teller to tell her information about her future.*

2. *Why did the woman come to speak with the fortune teller?*
   Quiere información sobre su futuro. = *She wants information about her future.*

3. *What does the ring in the crystal ball indicate?*
   Indica que la mujer se casará. = *They indicate that the woman will get married.*

4. *What will the fortune teller say about the future of the woman?*
   (Answers will vary but might include the following)
   La adivina dirá que la mujer se casará, viajará en un crucero, y que recibirá un coche nuevo. = *The fortune teller will say that the woman is going to get married, that she will travel on a cruise, and that she will get a new car.*

5. *Do you believe the woman's future will be good or bad? Why?*
   Creo que el futuro de la mujer será bueno porque sonríe. = *I believe the woman's future will be good because she is smiling.*

6. *Will the woman be happy with the prediction?*
   Sí la mujer estará contenta con la predicción. = *Yes the woman will be happy with the prediction.*

7. *What do the boat and car indicate?*
   Indican que la mujer viajará. = *They indicate that the woman will travel.*

8. *Why are there cards on the table?*
   La adivina usará las cartas para predecir lo que pasará en el futuro. = *The fortune teller will use the cards to predict what will happen in the future.*

Práctica 11.5
Answers will vary

Práctica 11.6
Answers will vary

Práctica 11.7

1. *Is the ceremony a wedding or a graduation?*
   Es una ceremonia de graduación. = *It's a graduation ceremony.*

2. *Is the young lady thinking about the past or the future?*
   Ella piensa en el futuro. = *She is thinking about the future.*

3. *Is this probably a student in high school or in the university?*
   (Answers will vary)

4. *Is the woman thinking about professions that she might have or about friends she met at the university?*
   Piensa en las profesiones que tendrá. = *She is thinking about professions she might have.*

5. *In the young lady's imagination, will she be an astronaut or a physicist?*
   En su imaginación, será astronauta. = *In her imagination, she will be an astronaut.*

6. *Will she maybe be a vet or a pediatrician?*
   Quizás será veterinaria. = *She will perhaps be a vet.*

7. *Will she maybe be a teacher or a bus driver?*
   Será conductora de autobús. = *She might be a bus driver.*

8. Do you believe the young lady will be successful in the future?
   Answers will vary.

Práctica 12.1

1. El jefe **requeriría** que los empleados completaran el trabajo.
   The boss would require that the employees completed the work.

2. Si fuéramos al restaurante, yo **pagaría** la cuenta.
   If we went to the restaurant, I would pay the bill.

3. Si las clases ocurrieran los jueves, los estudiantes **asistirían**.
   If the classes occurred on Thursdays, the students would attend.

4. ¿**Estarían** Uds. contentos si nosotros les diéramos más tarea?
   Would you all be content if we gave you all more homework?

5. ¿**Venderíais** vosotros los carros viejos?
   Would you guys sell the old cars?

6. Mis amigos y yo **nos sentaríamos** en la primera fila en la clase, pero los otros estudiantes ya estaban allí.
   My friends and I would sit in the first row of the class, but the other students were already there.

7. El doctor **leería** los resultados, pero el paciente no estaba allí.
   The doctor would read the results, but the patient wasn't there.

8. ¿**Traerías** tú las empanadas?
   Would you bring the empanadas?

9. **Sería** la una de la tarde cuando llegaron.
   It would be 1:00PM when they arrived.

10. Tú y yo **conoceríamos** a nuevos amigos si fuéramos a la fiesta.
    You and I would meet new friends if we went to the party.

11. Yo no **haría** eso si you fuera tú.
    I wouldn't do that if I were you.

12. **Nevaría** si hiciera más frío.
    It would snow if it were colder.

Práctica 12.2

1. Yo **habría** leído capítulo dos, pero yo no tenía tiempo.
   I would have read chapter two, but I didn't have time.

2. Nosotros **querríamos** practicar más.
   We would want to practice more.

3. Ana **saldría** a las ocho para llegar a tiempo.
   Ana would leave at 8:00 in order to arrive on time.

4. **Habría** muchos documentos para firmar.
   There would be many documents to sign.

5. Esa escultura **valdría** mucho dinero si pudiéramos comprarla.
   That sculpture would be worth a lot of money if we could buy it.

6. Creía que esos libros **cabrían** en el estante para libros.
   I believed that those books would fit on the bookshelf.

7. Uds. **habrían** escrito muchas de las palabras.
   You all would have written many of the words.

8. Yo creía que mi familia **podría** ir con Uds. al lago.
   I belived that my family could go with you all to the lake.

9. Yo no **sabría** jugar porque nunca **habría** jugado antes.
   I wouldn't know how to play because I would never have played before.

10. ¿**Tendrías** tú ganas de ir de compras mañana?
    Would you feel like going shopping tomorrow?

11. ¿**Vendrían** sus primos con nosotros?
    Would your (or his/her) cousins come with us?

12. ¿Quiénes **habrían** hecho reservaciones para nosotros?
    Who (all) would have made reservations for us?

13. ¿Le **dirías** tú mi secreto a Marta?
    Would you tell my secret to Martha?

14. Si tu novia viniera a cenar, ¿qué **querría** ella para comer?
    If your girlfriend came to eat dinner, what would she want to eat?

Práctica 12.3
1. *Who is the peron in the drawing?*
   La mujer es agente de viajes. = *The woman is a travel agent.*

2. *According to the travel agent, where should the person travel?*
   Según la agente de viajes, debería viajar a Puerto Rico. = *According to the travel agent, the person should travel to Puerto Rico.*

3. *What would a person see in Puerto Rico?*
   Vería playas, un bosque tropical, la fortaleza, y un coquí. = *A person would see beaches, a tropical rain forest, the fortress and a coquí (a small tree frog).*

4. *Would you sunbathe in Puerto Rico?*
   Sí, una persona tomaría el sol. = *Yes, a person would sunbathe.*

5. *On a trip to Puerto Rico, where would you find the coquí?*
   Encontrarías un coquí en el bosque tropical. = *You would see the coquí in the rain forest.*

6. *According to the poster, where would you go to learn a little history of Puerto Rico?*
   Irías a la fortaleza para aprender un poco de historia de Puerto Rico. = *You would go to the fortress to learn a little about the history of Puerto Rico.*

7. *Is there a lot of a little sightseeing in Puerto Rico?*
   Hay mucho para hacer turismo. = *There is a lot of sightseeing.*

8. *Would you talk with a travel agent to look for information about Puerto Rico?*
   Answers will vary.

Práctica 13.1

My name is Melissa. I was born in Glendale, California at the end of the 1960's. In my family there are my parents, my two older brothers, and myself. My dad was a lawyer and very hardworking. My mom was a housewife and always took care of us. I liked to spend time with my family. Generally, my family and I would go to a lake in the mountains to spend the weekends. I loved to fish, ride my bicycle or ride a motorcycle with my brother. Also during the summers, I liked to waterski. I was a very active young person and I spent a lot of time outside of the house. But my favorite activity was ice skating. I skated three times a week and sometimes I would compete in local competitions.

I was a very good student and my favorite subject was literature. When I was 16 years old, I traveled to Peru as an exchange student. There I learned a lot about the Peruvian people and culture. Culture fascinated me and I fell in love with the good, nice people there. Because of this experience I studied Spanish and literature in the university. I lived and studied in Mexico. I graduated and became a teacher in a high school in the community where I grew up.

I still love the Spanish language and the heritage Spanish speakers. I love to travel but I don't like to travel by plane. I'm afraid of flying in a plane. My marvelous husband and our kids spend a lot of time together. I like dogs a lot and I have two in my house. I walk them every day.

I would like to travel more in the future. Some day I will travel to Spain with my family. God willing I can travel to Peru also because I would like to reunite with my Peruvian family.

Práctica 13.2

Hi. How's everything going?

-So-so. I'm tired
-What a shame. Do you feel like resting?

-I'm well, thanks
-Very well. Do you want to watch a movie tonight?

-Yes
-Good. We can rent a movie and watch it in my house.

-No.
-Well, would you prefer to have dinner together?

-I would prefer to watch a movie in the theater.
-Do you want to see something special?

- It's a fabulous idea!
- Well, do you want to eat something special?

-The problem is that I don't have enough money.
- No problem. I'll treat you.

-No. But before leaving I have to get dressed.
-No problem. I'll wait for you. What time will you arrive?

- I will arrive at 8:00 PM at your house.
- ¡Uf! It's a little late. Could you arrive a little earlier?

- My car doesn't work. Could you pick me up?
- I have to get ready. Couldn't you walk?

- I don't think so. It's impossible.
- Good, then, I'll see you soon.

- I think so. I'll try to arrive at 6:00.
- Good. I'll see you at 6:00.

- Good. And would it be possible that you take me home afterwards?
- Yes, of course.

-You know what? After planning so much I don't have the energy to go out tonight.
- I understand. I feel the same.

- Thanks for inviting me. See you soon, right?
- Of course my friend. See you soon.

Práctica 13.3

14 Añada la lechuga y el tomate (Add lettuce and tomato)

3 Busque todos los ingredientes en el mercado (Look for the ingredients at the market)

16 Coma y disfrute el sándwich. (Eat and enjoy the sandwich)

5 Compre los ingredientes en el supermercado. (Buy the ingredients in the supermarket)

1 Haga una lista de las cosas que necesitas. (Make a list of the things that you need)

7 Lave la lechuga y el tomate. (Wash the lettuce and the tomato)

6 Lleve todo lo que necesita a la casa. (Take everything you need to the house)

12 Ponga el jamón sobre el pan. (Put the ham on top of the bread)

15 Ponga el otro pedazo de pan encima de todo. (Put the other piece of bread on top of everything)

9 Ponga el pan en un plato (Put the bread on a plate)

13 Ponga el queso encima del jamón. (Put the cheese on top of the ham)

4 Ponga todos los ingredientes en el carrito. (Put all the ingredients in the cart)

8 Ponga todos los ingredientes en el mostrador. (Put all the ingredients on the counter)

10 Unte la mayonesa en el pan con el cuchillo. No ponga demasiado. (Spread the mayonnaise on the bread with the knife. Don't put too much.)

11 Unte la mostaza en el pan. (Spread the mustard on the bread)

2 Vaya al supermercado. (Go to the supermarket)

Práctica 13.4

La semana pasada yo visité a mis primos en San Francisco. Yo no los había visto por muchos años. Mi primo, Eduardo celebraba su cumpleaños de treinta años y yo quería estar allí para celebrar con él. Hace un mes mi tía y tío me dijeron que ellos le darían una fiesta para Eduardo y me rogaron venir. Pero no tenían que rogar. Fue un placer ir.

Durante la semana en San Francisco, yo celebré el cumpleaños, pero también (yo) hice muchas otras actividades. Yo pasé tiempo con mi tía, mi tío, y primos cuando me llevaron al muelle y a un restaurante elegante en el pueblo chino. Nosotros fuimos a Alacatraz y me llevaron en su coche sobre el Puente Golden Gate. Yo comí mucho del pan delicioso.

Yo me divertí mucho con mi familia durante la semana en San Francisco, y me gustaría visitarlos otra vez muy pronto.

Práctica 13.5

To Whom It May Concern:

I would like to travel to Puerto Rico, but I need help with the preparations for the trip. I will travel with my husband and my two kids. My children are eight and eleven years old. We want to travel with commercial airlines and we would prefer a direct flight.

In Puerto Rico we will need a room with two or three beds. One of the beds will have to be a king-sized bed. The other can be a queen or better, two twin beds.

It's necessary that the hotel be near the beach. We hope to visit the Fortress El Morro, the town center, and various sites of interest, but we will spend the majority of the time playing at the beach and sunbathing. If you have a map, please show it to me because I would like to know where the tourist sites are in relation to the hotel site.

Thank you in advance,
Mrs. O'Gara

Práctica 13.6

A quien corresponda:

A mi esposa y a mí nos gustaría viajar a varias ciudades y sitios de interés en Perú. Nos gustaría si Ud. nos ayudara hacer preparativos para este viaje. Nosotros viajaremos en el mes de agosto porque será el invierno en Perú y el verano en Los Estados Unidos. Tenemos tres semanas de vacaciones durante el mes de agosto.

Nos gustaría visitar a Lima, Cuzco, y a Macchu Pichu. ¿Nos podría recomendar unos hoteles? Nos gustaría las habitaciones que tengan una cama de matrimonio extra grande. Preferiríamos hoteles de tres estrellas or más. Es muy importante que los hoteles estén en el centro comercial porque no alquilaremos ningún coche y tendremos que tomar autobuses.

Gracias de antemano,
Sr. Salinas

Práctica 13.7

1. _E_ Si yo fuera tú, visitaría el Museo Nacional.

A. I hope that it doesn't rain nor that it's too hot either.

2. _I_ Yo quisiera que Ud. corte los arbustos.

B. I am glad that you all are here.

3. _B_ Me alegro de que Uds. estén aquí.

C. I visited Mexico three years ago.

4. _G_ No me gusta que tú no me digas la verdad.

D. She doubts that we will arrive on time.

5. _A_ Ojalá que no llueva ni que tampoco haga calor.

E. If I were you, I'd visit the National Museum.

6. _J_ Por favor, no hable tan rápido.

F. It's important that you read it before signing.

7. _C_ Yo visité a México hace tres años.

G. I don't like that you're not telling me the truth.

8. _F_ Es importante que tú lo leas antes de firmar.

H. It's obvious that I understand Spanish well.

9. _D_ Ella duda que lleguemos a tiempo.

I. I would like you to cut the bushes.

10. _H_ Es obvio que yo comprendo bien el español.

J. Please don't speak so quickly.

Práctica 13.8

My brother and I traveled to Europe last year. Art fascinates him and he wanted to go to France to visit the Louvre. While he was traveling through Paris, he decided to take a train to Spain. He had time and although he was having fun in France, he wanted to see the Spanish architecture of Spain.

He knew that the trains left often for Spain. He decided to take the train on Monday in the morning. He boarded the high-speed train at 6:00AM and arrived in Barcelona at 12:30PM. The train traveled at 200 miles per hour! It was incredible and very efficient.

Práctica 13.9

Dear Michael,

Greetings from Mexico DF! I hope that this card finds you in good health.

I've been here in the capital of Mexico for one week and I'm having a lot of fun. I want you to be here with me. But I know that you still have classes in the university. Some day you will have to visit this incredible and beautiful city.

I have done a lot during my first week here. First, some friends of the program recommended to me that I stay in a hotel near the town center. It was an excellent recommendation because it's a perfect hotel for me. The employees are very friendly and helpful. I visited the Zócalo, the main square, and the Fine Arts Palace. I took a bus and I went to Teotihuacán. It was a magnificent and very interesting place. I learned a lot about the history of Mexico although nobody knows who built that original city. I took a ton of photos of the Pyramid of the Sun and the Pyramid of the Moon.

In the upcoming week, I will visit the Museum of Anthropology and I will talk with some students from the University Autónoma to learn more about life today in Mexico City.

When I return to Miami, we will have to go get coffee. I can show you my photos and talk about my experience in this country.

Take care and write me. I would like to receive news from you. I miss you a lot. Hugs and kisses to all!

With much love,
Susana

Práctica 13.10

Querida Melissa,

¡Saludos de Glendale, California! Ojalá que esta carta te encuentre de buena salud. Yo he estudiado español en mi clase por seis semanas, y me divierto mucho.

Cada día yo estudio español. Yo aprendo mucho en mis clases, pero aprendo más cuando hablo con mis amigos nuevos. Yo he conocido a unos amigos nuevos porque hablamos mucho en nuestra clase. Hablamos de nuestras vidas y de las cosas que nos gustan y no nos gustan. Me alegro de que podamos hablar y pasar tiempo juntos. Ellos son muy simpáticos y amables.

Mi maestro nos pide que estudiemos fuera de la clase. ¡Hay mucho que aprender! ¡Pero ya yo sé hablar español muy bien!

En las semanas entrantes, yo continuaré a estudiar y hablar español. Ojalá que yo pueda practicar mi español con muchos hispanohablantes. ¿Hablarás conmigo y me ayudarás? Yo sé que tú hablas español bien también. Nosotros tendremos que ir a cenar o a tomar café para que practiquemos juntos.

¡Escríbeme pronto! ¡Te extraño mucho! ¡Abrazos y besos a la familia!

Con cariño,
Tu Amigo(a)

¡Bien hecho!

Made in the USA
San Bernardino, CA
05 April 2018